THE PROBLEM OF FREEDOM IN POSTMODERN EDUCATION

Critical Studies in Education and Culture Series

The Politics of Education: Culture, Power and Liberation
Paulo Freire

Popular Culture, Schooling and the Language of Everyday Life
Henry A. Giroux and Roger I. Simon

Teachers As Intellectuals: Toward a Critical Pedagogy of Learning
Henry A. Giroux

Women Teaching for Change: Gender, Class and Power
Kathleen Weiler

Between Capitalism and Democracy: Educational Policy and the Crisis of the Welfare State
Svi Shapiro

Critical Psychology and Pedagogy: Interpretation of the Personal World
Edmund Sullivan

Pedagogy and the Struggle for Voice: Issues of Language, Power, and Schooling for Puerto Ricans
Catherine E. Walsh

Learning Work: A Critical Pedagogy of Work Education
Roger I. Simon, Don Dippo, and Arleen Schenke

Cultural Pedagogy: Art/Education/Politics
David Trend

Raising Curtains on Education: Drama as a Site for Critical Pedagogy
Clar Doyle

Toward a Critical Politics of Teacher Thinking: Mapping the Postmodern
Joe L. Kincheloe

Building Communities of Difference: Higher Education in the Twenty-First Century
William G. Tierney

The Problem of Freedom in Postmodern Education

TOMASZ SZKUDLAREK

CRITICAL STUDIES IN EDUCATION AND CULTURE SERIES
Edited by
HENRY A. GIROUX AND PAULO FREIRE

BERGIN & GARVEY
Westport, Connecticut • London

Library of Congress Cataloging-in-Publication Data

Szkudlarek, Tomasz.
    The problem of freedom in postmodern education / Tomasz
Szkudlarek.
        p.   cm. — (Critical studies in education and culture series,
    ISSN 1064–8615)
    Includes bibliographical references and index.
    ISBN 0–89789–322–0. — ISBN 0–89789–323–9 (pbk.)
        1. Education—Political aspects.   2. Critical pedagogy.
    3. Education—Social aspects.   4. Liberty.   5. Deconstruction.
    I. Title.   II. Series.
    LC71.S97   1993
    370.11—dc20   92–39122

British Library Cataloguing in Publication Data is available.

Library of Congress Catalog Card Number: 92–39122
ISBN: 0–89789–322–0
        0–89789–323–9 (pbk.)
ISSN: 1064–8615

First published in 1993

Bergin & Garvey, 88 Post Road West, Westport, CT 06881
An imprint of Greenwood Publishing Group, Inc.

Printed in the United States of America

∞™

The paper used in this book complies with the
Permanent Paper Standard issued by the National
Information Standards Organization (Z39.48–1984).

10 9 8 7 6 5 4 3 2 1

LC
71
.S97
.1993

Contents

Series Foreword: Border Identities and the Practice of Freedom

Postmodernism is no longer fashionable. In fact, in some theoretical quarters it is seen as an outright reactionary plunge into the abyss of either a playful aesthetic or a free-floating textuality. For the most part, the debate about the meaning and significance of postmodern discourses has been waged primarily among intellectuals from the Western-style democracies. As invigorating as this debate has been, there has been a curious absence of discussion regarding the relevance of postmodern social criticism for understanding the collapse of communism in Eastern Europe and the former Soviet Union. This is all the more interesting since such a collapse appears to further the notion that we are living in a world in which the conditions of social life are in a stage of a fundamental transformation, fragmentation, and destabilization. The new world order that is emerging is being reconstructed between and outside of old borders, and the global space that is being configured can no longer be defined through modernist categories.

In this book Tomasz Szkudlarek has assumed the role of a border intellectual travelling between the rapidly disintegrating borders of the Soviet-dominated Polish state and its traditional other, the United States. Recognizing that as a border crosser, he is rewriting

his own identity, Szkudlarek does more than take up the relationship between identity and difference as the intersection of multiple
subject positions, or as the assertion of contingency and plurality.
Szkudlarek's journey into difference follows a route that is un-
charted by most Western intellectuals and educators. He takes on
the task of writing politics back into the postmodern, but he does
so in order to deepen the very notion of human agency and
collective struggle by engaging the political as the discourse of
freedom. For Szkudlarek, the domain of the political can only be
mapped through an analysis of the ideological, cultural, and material formations that limit or enable the capacities human beings
have to understand and transform the conditions of their own
existence. More specifically, Szkudlarek wants to extend the importance of the pedagogical by linking it to a concept of emancipation defined through the interrelated discourses of freedom and
identity formation. In this case Szkudlarek wants to move between
the borders of the East and the West in order to further understand
how pedagogy instructs identity formation and how identity formation instructs the practice of freedom.

But the crucial recognition that all forms of eduction presuppose
a notion of freedom and engage in the construction of identities is
not simply asserted by Szkudlarek. In a brilliant attempt to ground
theory and practice in forms of analysis that are at once historical,
semiotic, and transformative, Szkudlarek traces the relationship
between freedom and identity in the discourses of traditional
modernism, liberal capitalist ideology, and the radical discourses
of poststructuralism, postmodernism, and postcolonialism. For
Szkudlarek, while it is important to recognize that education is
about freedom and power, it is crucial to address what type of
freedom is at stake in the intersection of identity, power, language,
and history. Rejecting the traditional notion of freedom as being
synonymous with the logic of choice that informs the market or
the liberal reduction of freedom to the rights of individuals,
Szkudlarek charts a notion of freedom that is at once social, ethical,
collective, resistant, and deeply aware of the dialectics of power.

Moving between the educational borderlands forged in the East and the West, Szkudlarek analyzes how the dynamics of freedom and identity formation manifest themselves across pedagogical, educational, and cultural differences. Boldly asserting the need for a politics of difference in which otherness becomes hybridized rather than polarized, Szkudlarek posits how the dynamics of freedom and identity, when linked to a critical pedagogical practice, hold democracy responsible for its radical possibilities. In this Szkudlarek begins to outline the dynamics of a pedagogical practice in which freedom and identity became the starting point for developing alternative cartographies of desire, language, and identity. Szkudlarek engages his readers as one who has experienced the borderization of a society in which East and West mutually pervade each other. But Szkudlarek wants to refigure how identities are to be framed within the intersecting cultural pedagogies of the East and the West. Rejecting differences that consume the other, that exist in relations of domination and commercialization, Szkudlarek argues for a practice and project of freedom in which there is no fixed, authoritative meaning, negotiation is contingent upon the recognition that surplus meanings will always exist, and agency never forgets the extent to which it is beset by horrors that can be addressed and transformed.

Szkudlarek is a border intellectual inspired by a postmodern utopianism and encouraged by the legacies of postcolonial resistance. He believes and demonstrates that pedagogy is not merely about policing and domination. In spite of his own experiences under the grip of a repressive police state in which borders became an expression of violence and zones of separation, Szkudlarek has been able to create a view of pedagogy and schooling that serves as a borderland of hybrid possibilities, as a site of crossing that deterritorializes culture in the service of a project of human freedom that provides the basis for agency, struggle, and transformation. This is a book that will be read by those educators and cultural workers who want to understand how pedagogy as a form of cultural politics can serve to open up a new dialogue between the East and the West, and to engage a new model of self-criticism in which othering becomes less an attack on difference than a recognition of the ethical imperative to address and construct difference as a third space where new possibilities for human justice and a multicultural democracy can be realized.

Henry A. Giroux

Acknowledgments

This book was written mainly during my stay at Miami University in Oxford, Ohio, where I had a unique opportunity to study and work in the Center for Education and Cultural Studies, then run by Professor Henry Giroux, to whom I express my deepest gratitude for his teaching, friendship, and wisdom. I also give my warmest thanks to Professor Peter McLaren, then associate director and now director of the Center, for his friendship and many inspirations. I want to thank Professor Nelda McCabe, the chair of the Department of Educational Leadership, the members of the faculty of the department, and Jo Rosenberg from the Office of International Programs of Miami University for their hospitality and support and for the excellent conditions they created for my work. I express my thanks to the Kosciuszko Foundation, New York, which sponsored my visit to Miami University and my research on this book. My project could not have been completed without my friends who supported me and made my stay in the United States a fantastic experience. I want to thank Jeanne Giroux-Brady, Jane McLaren, Professor Dennis Carlson, David Trend, Martin O'Neil, Barry Nedelman, Khaula Murtadha, Chris and Suellyn Henke, Jennifer Berkshire, and all the doctoral students from the center. I also thank my wife, Anna, and my children, Maciek and Asia, for their understanding. I give my special thanks to my editors, Sophie Craze, Lynn Flint, Charles Eberline, and Alicia Merritt, for their support and excellent cooperation.

THE PROBLEM OF
FREEDOM IN POSTMODERN
EDUCATION

Chapter One

East-West, Right-Left: Postmodernism, Postsocialism, and the Problem of Education

"Well, you see," said one of the disputants at the 1991 University Council for Educational Administration Annual Conference in Baltimore, "there must be something good about our educational system!" The astonishment was expressed in reaction to the presentation of a delegate from Byelorussia, who outlined a project of educational reform in the former Soviet republic grounded in notions of school-based management, individual freedom of students and teachers, "happiness" in a stress-free environment, IQ and achievement testing, and other "purely American" educational inventions. The presentation was titled "In the High Hope of Cooperation."[1]

Similar astonishment appears in reactions of my students in Gdansk, Poland, when they read about Americans who attempted to improve their educational system in the aftermath of the Sputnik shock by emulating some features of Soviet pedagogy. Does that mean that there was "something good" about the hated Soviet-style school remembered by my students from their childhood? Certainly some interesting dynamics of (mis)interpretation are at play here, and they are visible on both sides of the former Iron Curtain.

Present "high hopes of cooperation" between East and West are vain if we do not learn to understand them.

The hope of cooperation with the West has definitely been a major factor in East European revolutions, an incentive to act, a utopian horizon of alternative thinking. In educational reforms like the Byelorussian one, this hope is based on the belief that the West means freedom and wealth; this belief creates expectations that American expertise and technology will solve tremendous problems resulting from the devastating outcomes of the Communist monopoly in social politics, that the former East can easily become westernized, and that Western values and technologies are real panaceas to Eastern problems. It is just another version of the economic infatuation with liberal market capitalism, thought to be the remedy for all social problems.

Hopes for cooperation are being expressed in the West as well, although they seem to be driven mainly by the fear of uncontrolled proliferation of Soviet nuclear weapons. Whatever the motives, however realistic the expectations, for the first time in the history of the two-bloc power system (and for the last time as well, as this system is disappearing) there is a chance, and a real challenge, of cooperation. Now and then somebody ponders whether we can live up to the challenge, or whether we will miss the unique opportunity to actively shape the future of a vast part of the world so as to make it a more bearable place to live. That is not going to be an easy thing to do or even to think about. One of the most profound results of the fall of the Berlin Wall, and probably the most difficult to overcome, is the deep identity crisis of former enemies now facing the challenge of cooperation. The crisis involves a triple process of "othering," of creating the other who may serve the need of establishing, in contrast, one's own identity. First, the West and the East, safely separated by the wall during their formative years, developed images of each other rather remote from what respective sides tend to think about themselves. These are two "others"; the third is just being created by the unifying Euro-American hybrid that is trying to shape its identity in contrast to some other culture, some other political structure and military alliance. "Who is the enemy?" seems to be one of the most urgent and disquieting questions in the age when "everybody" wants to enter NATO— everybody except those others. Everything seems to point to the Third World as the scapegoat of this process of identity formation. People of Africa, of the Middle East, and of Asia are being "othered" wherever they are, in their own countries and when they arrive in the West. Europe, "going multicultural," is on the verge of developing its own version of apartheid in the name of multicultural diversity. The growing popularity of ultra-Right political movements in France or Germany would be a good example here. In Eastern Europe there are still some active old areas of conflict that provide for sad possibilities of experimenting with new identities, mostly concentrated around nationalistic tensions, but as soon as these are exhausted—or even before, in order to exhaust them—Eastern Europe will also join the chorus of the West searching for aliens who do not want to join NATO.

The processes of othering—the old one, concerning "my part of the world" in relation to the Iron Curtain, and the new one, slowly yet inevitably replacing the East-West dimension with the North-South one—urgently need intellectual effort if we are to understand anything of the challenges to the identity (or rather identities) of the contemporary world, where all distinctions and borders are becoming more and more blurred. There is no clear border between collective and individual identities, between politics and education, between personal development and cultural change. There is no clear border between former blocs of the East and the West; there is no clear border, either, between the oppositional ideologies elaborated thus far on respective sides of the Iron Curtain. It seems of prime importance that we somehow understand the processes that are currently taking place in such a deterritorialized, border-free world (or rather one totally included within the border) before our "borderlands" freeze in new ideologies, in new identities, in new, taken-for-granted, obvious maps of "the same" and "the other." How can this be done?

In the following presentation I will concentrate on educational issues (education is one of the "borderlands" itself, crisscrossing all possible dimensions of identity, culture, and politics). I will try to sketch a kind of "ideological map of educational discourses" and to find out how we can grasp a notion of freedom inherent in educational philosophies. This notion creates a broad perspective in which issues of politics, culture, and identity formation can be analyzed with clear reference to recent changes in the world. I will mostly concentrate on American educational theories, as these are my "other" ways of thinking. I will try to understand them in their broad dimensions, so that a common ground of "border discourse" can somehow be defined. But first I will have to deal with the very problem of otherness as it has been shaped by the cold war experience. Before we construct a common "borderland" providing for a kind of shelter for the East and the West, we have to draw an outline of "commonness" in our respective otherness. We have to understand how similar we are in our differences, and how different we are in what sounds the same. Having imagined this provisionally blueprinted common ground, I will turn it into a background for the analysis of freedom and identity formation in educational practices and thus open up the question of the new challenges to identity construction, which inevitably imply some "secondary" othering, some new dimensions of the same old game of power. I hope that this journey will make me understand something of what is going on in the postmodern, postsocialist, postcolonial, postindustrial, and post-whatever world that has not found its positive identity yet. I would like to understand this before the process is done, before we create Our Great Common Other who will define our borders.

EAST-WEST, RIGHT-LEFT: A HORIZONTAL GEOGRAPHY OF DISCOURSE

Just as American disputants were astonished by the presentation of their Byelorussian colleague, he felt shocked, as he told me, by the opening address of the conference delivered by Henry A. Giroux.[2] Giroux's presentation called for a new ethical and political language of theorizing that would open up the way for democratic education in the United States. The very idea of the discourse of education being political was threatening to the Byelorussian guest of the conference; even more threatening were clearly visible references to the discourse of the Left in Giroux's presentation. How can we explain this strange combination of misunderstandings? And how, with these misunderstandings, can we think of a common ground in emancipatory theorizing? In their background, as it seems, there is a more general problem of identity formation in relation to otherness.

One of the most influential definitions of the contemporary claims that we live in a transitional period of "postmodern" culture.[3] Modern ideas of reason, progress, individual autonomy, nation, and science—all founding myths of Western civilization— have exhausted their legitimizing power, ceased to provide visions justifying social agency, and failed to outline a horizon of hope for a world in permanent crisis. Reasons for that demise of Reason have been identified on various levels. The revolution in communication made the idea of centered, hierarchical knowledge production irrelevant. The world accessible through electronic media is decentered, multidimensional, and always partial. Moreover, it is increasingly difficult to say what the world is at all. The world seems to be confined to images produced in popular culture, no longer distinguishable from the traditional, "high" culture; the world is in images referring to other images, continuously repeating tropes, visions, and fragments of other images. The world has become a "simulacrum," a copy without an original, an image hiding the lack of the original.[4] In a strange way this cultural phenomenon coincides with the worldview developed in the contemporary physical sciences, where relativism, methodological anarchism, and the notion of the world being constructed rather than discovered in course of scientific experiments settled down for good. Visible, centered subjects of rational decisions disappear also as the economy loses its national character and more and more involves globally operating, multinational, and virtually uncontrollable corporations. What has also changed is the very way the economy seems to operate. Industrial production abandons "developed" countries and goes where cheap labor is; the West is left with a kind of mixture of services and financial institutions producing money instead of goods—another kind of simulacra, signs with no referents, copies without "real" objects.

All these phenomena are reflected in the domain of politics. Multinationalism, the demise of the significance of the nation as a center of politics, global challenges (nuclear threat, multinational recession, ecology), and the shaky balance of power relations all have to do with the way the world is understood. With the crisis of science and ideological hegemony, with the demise of "master narratives" of the past, world politics seems to lack legitimizing ideas; it is more and more difficult to justify political action in moral or rational terms. Power has become naked, unprotected by ethical claims, visible, and overtly interest-oriented. Through its decentration it is also becoming more and more a matter of everyday life. It affects people not involved directly in any kind of political (in the traditional sense) institutions. Politics is everywhere: in the home, in the media, and in the school, as well as in governmental institutions. On the one hand, this process makes it possible to politically articulate areas of oppression that were invisible in the centralized, modernist political culture (like gender-, age-, and sexual-orientation-based exclusions and domination), but on the other, it opened up the way to political terrorism. If power is everywhere, if it permeates everyday social life, it seems "reasonable" to target at random innocent people, as they are thought to be bearers of oppressive domination. Terrorism is part of a much broader "politics of inclusions," of charging collective subjects (nations, genders, races, or religions) with responsibility for somebody's oppression. Such "collectivization" of agency and responsibility in a world where no individual agents can be made responsible for social oppression can also be seen on the formal, institutional level of politics. We are witnessing a growing wave of populism addressing everyday issues in a "horizontal" way, from the perspective of popular beliefs and stereotypes, without any references to broader or deeper political visions grounded in traditional ideologies.

Postmodernism, apart from marking the end of modernism, clearly opens up some new cultural perspective. It is a new discourse, a new way of understanding the world. It has already gained a kind of theoretical self-consciousness in spite of its "refusal" to name itself with a "positive" label not including a referent to the epoch that is being challenged. In the social sciences the new understanding involves new languages brought about by poststructural philosophy, first of all by theories developed by Jacques Derrida and Michel Foucault.

Derrida's philosophy can be considered as a step ahead from Heidegger's critique of metaphysics. While Heidegger disclosed the notion of Being, of the holistic process in which all particular beings, with their apparent dualistic oppositions, are grounded, Derrida found that there is a rule prior to Being, "older" than Being, a rule preceding the very possibility of existence. That rule "is not" in an ontological sense, but it makes Being possible. Derrida calls that rule *différance*, and the word covers numerous notions speaking to the possibility of being. In order to be, one has to differ, to defer, to detour; being is nondirect and implies meaning that appears with a delay of representation, with substituting one thing for another. Such a notion opposes the metaphysical tradition (the logocentric tradition, as Derrida calls it) based upon the premise of the priority of "directness" and therefore on the priority of speaking over writing. Speech, in that tradition, seems to be more directly linked to the "pure experience" grounded in the language, in the word, in Logos perceived as directly linked to the nature of being. Writing, then, seems secondary, supplementary, unauthentic. But, as Derrida points out, any meaning must imply a kind of indirectness, a delay, a detour; *différance* then, is fundamental to meaning. Writing, as its nature is based on substitution, on difference, is prior to speaking, for it is in the play of differences, constitutive of writing, that meanings are forged. Moreover, there is no meaning outside differences. Meaning appears in a constant play of significants that cannot be related to anything outside the text. One of the results of this idea is the thesis that metalanguage, which could serve the need of distancing the reader from the language in order to interrogate its claims and meanings, is impossible. The only way left for critical thinking, then, is *deconstruction* of the language undertaken *from within*. How is this possible?

Derrida notes that meanings are "paired," that concepts we use are organized in oppositional dualistic structures. These oppositions constitute the structure of meaning in an active way; that is, not only do they set one concept against another, but they define exclusions as well, they decide what can and what cannot be said in the language. Moreover, it is usually the case that the first concept in a pair is charged with positive value, whereas the second one plays the role of a contrasting "supplement," a negative, a reversal. Good is "not bad," white is "not black," big is "not small." In the process of identity construction we tend to identify ourselves with the "good" side of linguistically constructed meanings, excluding the rest as "the other"; "otherness" is thus constructed as the very negative of our identities. It is here that the whole process of signification is opened up to power relations, to the sphere of politics. To deconstruct the language—which, in this context, means as well to conduct a political critique, to interrogate value judgments and the process of identity formation—one has to break the structure of meaning. This is possible, because not all concepts fit into the dualistic scheme. The task of the critic, then, is to find these "undecidables," the concepts that are the "neither nor" of the language, that break out of its structure and open up a space of different articulation. Deconstruction, which is not directly a political critique, therefore has political significance.[5]

If the work of Derrida is grounded in the critique of language, Foucault's stems from the analysis of history. As Foucault concluded on his own work, the main issues he was concerned with were power and knowledge in their mutual relations.[6] His last lectures and writings added the notion of subjectivity to those central categories.[7]

Traditional investigations into the issue of power concern how power is established in the discourse of truth. Foucault reverses this relation and focuses on the issue of truth (knowledge) being produced in the discourse of power. Truth and knowledge prove here to be instruments of power rather than its source. One of the crucial aspects of this theory is the notion of decentered power relations. Power is not merely confined to "vertical" social dimensions; it is "horizontal," that is, it is carried on by the people who themselves are subject to power. The process of establishing power relations consists of a kind of colonization: the state, or some other sovereign political agent, appropriates mechanisms of control developed in everyday social relations, in institutions dealing with crime, illness, education, and other forms of dependence. Techniques of surveillance, developed to control juvenile sexuality, work efficiency of prisoners, and other behaviors of people in a situation of subordination, have been charged with ideologically "progressive" values and have replaced mechanisms of repression that previously dominated the sphere of political power. In his classic analysis of Jeremy Bentham's *Panopticon*, Foucault shows how surveillance acts as a positive kind of power, not just restricting people from certain behaviors but producing their subjectivities. The crucial moment of control here is constituted by the process of distribution of knowledge: Panopticon is so designed that its inhabitants do not know when their behavior is observed. A concentric building, with a central well where the rooms of the supervisors are located, makes it possible for the supervisors to see their dependents without being seen by them. In such a situation inhabitants (prisoners, patients, students, and so on) have to behave as if they were observed all the time. In this way they interiorize the gaze, the mechanism of control, and construct their subjectivities in accordance with the expectations of their supervisors. Subjugation, says Foucault, is the act of subjectivity production.

So "produced," subjects can themselves play roles of supervisors in relations with other people. Having interiorized the demands of power, they execute power in social life. Power becomes dispersed, decentered, circular, spread in chainlike structures all over the society. What keeps this structure alive, what makes it coherent and self-reproducing, is the production of discourse in relations of power. What is knowledge and what is not, what is truth and what is not, is defined in circular power relations. Knowledge is inscribed into everyday practices; social relations maintain the criteria of distinguishing between truth and un-truth, reason and un-reason. With subjectivities constructed in this way, there is no need for the system to maintain visible, spectacular agencies of power (public trials and executions, torture, physical repression). Discipline takes over; power becomes invisible, silent, tacit, inscribed into everyday activities, into popular knowledge, into the bodies of the subjects. Politics, since the eighteenth century, when disciplinary power took over, can be decentered, can comprise everyday activities without a threat of destabilizing the whole mechanism of social control. Human rights can be made a public issue; legal protection of an individual can become a standard of the social life, because it is not the Law, not repression, not legal requirements, not rights, not individual freedom from physical oppression that make the system tick. The discourse of rights hides the fundamental mechanism of power. Constant, silent surveillance carried on by individuals educated under the gaze of power is made invisible by the dominant ideology of individual rights.

As we can see, both these philosophies account for practically all basic dimensions of postmodernity. Decentration of power, the demise of autonomous subjectivity, the "crisis of representation" expressed in the notion of meaning as a play of signifiers, and the prior role of difference in social ontology have their significant theoretical articulation in the writings of Foucault and Derrida. The importance of these writings has become particularly clear through their reception and appropriation in the discourse of politics. The critical potential of Foucault's notion of power made it possible to articulate the politics of the everyday; the Derridean notion of *différance* made it possible to justify pluralistic visions of identity construction and made subversive claims of feminism, countering the male, "invisible" domination in the name of "sameness," philosophically sound. Theoretically refined postmodernism has become a significant ground for social criticism and alternative thinking in politics, aesthetics, education, and practically the whole scope of social research.

How do these notions translate themselves into the perspective of postsocialist countries? What do these countries have in common with this "cultural logic of late capitalism," as Frederic Jameson defined postmodernism,[8] when they are just trying to introduce market economies after half a century of Communist rule? How can leftist articulations of the postmodern discourse be of any significance in the East, just trying to free itself from interiorized leftist ideologies that delay its "march to freedom and prosperity"? If we are to find any grounds for talking about "new times"[9] in common terms, we have to search for similarities, however unlikely it seems that they can be found at first.

One of the important features of postmodern culture is its superficiality: the surface, appearance, seems to be more important than the depth. Differences—and differences are significant—are displayed on the surface of reality. So are similarities. This does not mean that there is no point in comparing deep, structural features of the systems. I will try to compare both surfaces and structures, although it is very difficult to describe surfaces. Their contingent, unstructured, and almost liquid nature makes it very difficult to use verbal means of representation in a relevant way. A text like this is perhaps the worst possible setting for accounts of surfaces. Surfaces are "filmable," structures are "writable." (Once again we can see here an element of coherence in the partial, contingent, and diversified culture of postmodernism: the stress on surfaces goes hand in hand with the domination of visual media.) What I can do here is to write about surfaces in a structured way, so as to incorporate them into a "writable" relation. The point is that surfaces of the East are getting similar to those of the West in a surprisingly rapid way. It is as if the only outcome (definitely the only visible outcome) of the anti-Communist revolution was the similarity of the surface. This is not a trivial thing. In a world where power is exercised through gaze, and where power constructs subjectivities, people's identities must depend on looks. I will write about this process in a more detailed way later on, discussing the issue of identity construction in relation to power.

I wonder if middle-class American readers can imagine a socialist world where people were deprived of all possibilities of acquiring visual signs of acclaimed social status, where there was no market for desired, "good," "quality" identity clues, where almost all one could buy was stigmatized as worse, obsolete, secondhand, and poor. I wonder if these readers can imagine what it meant to be deprived of all signs of the dominant culture, to be visibly marginalized—by clothes, by cars, by housing designs—on a national scale. People could see images of "America" in movie theatres, they read their hidden normative message ("If you want to be free, you have to wear . . . , walk . . . , drink . . . , eat . . . ," and so on), and they had no possibilities to construct their identities (that is, their appearances) in a way that would have made them "belong," feel "the same," feel "not worse." This is why they could spend a month's income on a pair of jeans; this is why people in Moscow can stand in line for hours to get their "Big Mac" and "feel American." This is why in bars where I used to drink beer there were always displays of colorful cigarette ads, even though there were no cigarettes to buy. The feeling people were striving for was the feeling of belonging, of not being the other. The colonial message concerning which culture is "better" and which one is "worse" was read immediately, and it significantly influenced people's everyday appearances. The subjugation of East European countries was, therefore, twofold. In terms of macropolitics they were subordinate to the USSR; in terms of everyday culture, of popular images creating patterns of desire and thus shaping people's identities, they were subordinate to the West.

With political liberalization and the introduction of market economies, the surface of the West flooded the streets of East European countries. Nowadays everybody can look, eat, drink, and walk American, provided she or he has the money. The question appears here whether this unification of surfaces has any deeper meaning, whether it means that we can really speak in terms of cultural unification opening the East for postmodern culture. To put it in another way, this is the question of relations between surfaces and structures, the question whether the surface phenomena can soak into social and political structures in a way that would affect long-term processes.

In my opinion, we are witnessing a deeply permeating process of cultural colonization taking place in Eastern Europe as the change of surfaces, or rather the change proceeding from the surface, meets deep structural phenomena that seem to have prepared the ground for instant "postmodernization" of the East. Note how similar the process of signification in the example of people in Eastern Europe attempting to construct their visual identifications in relation to Western culture, is to the process described by Western theorists of the media. Signs refer to other signs; they represent not "real" things but images (clothes like those seen in the movie). But this phenomenon was not the first simulacrum in the culture of the East. The signifying structure was prepared there by political propaganda and by spectacular events like May First parades (Working Class Day) or elections with one candidate to choose. Huge propaganda billboards were advertising political parties as if there was a possibility of choice and public support was crucial to their power; they displayed commonplace truths (like "We want to live in peace") or smart lies (like "The Warsaw Treaty is a warranty of our security," which was true if you thought of the possibility of a direct Soviet military intervention in case, say, of a country that would want to become neutral). People were reading these things, were writing them (artists were well paid for this kind of creativity), were saying them, and did not mean them. Signs did not relate to any extratextual reality; they were creating their own domain of pure textuality, their own world marked with special "opening" clues (the red background of propaganda billboards, the unique syntax of sentences that peculiarly avoided verbs, certain graphic logos) acting as warnings, as "don't mean it" messages. The political spectacle had only one real referent: participation. You had to take part, to be present, to be seen on particular days in particular places. On the one hand, it was a powerful means of surveillance, forcing people to interiorize "benign" aspects of totalitarian mentality ("I was there but I didn't mean it"); on the other, it taught people to be very attentive in distinguishing messages that had extratextual reference from those that did not and thus contributed to the emergence of "social schizophrenia," of a multiplicity of subject positions from which people were acting and speaking. Just as they were meaning certain texts and not meaning others, they were behaving in relevant manners in particular public and private spaces. They could easily say things they did not mean in places where they were just seen, be they courtrooms, classrooms, or Communist party meetings. They could work on *nomenklatura* positions (those approved by the Communist party) and identify themselves with opposition movements. Words went with places of enunciation, actions with institutions, not with conscious identities. Such a displacement of subjectivity created in turn a unique structure of value perception.

In his impressive research into value systems of the Polish society of the 1970s, Stefan Nowak identified a number of features characteristic of the late phase of socialist society on the verge of revolution (massive strikes in the year 1980 gave birth to the Solidarity movement that eventually, nine years later, brought an end to communism).[10] Nowak found a deep discrepancy between attitudes to the socialist reality (predominantly negative) and the criteria of judgments concerning that reality: the criteria were socialist, and were taken over from official educational and political messages. This means that people interiorized socialist standards that were established to legitimize the party's power and used them to criticize the socialist reality. Paradoxically, the Communist propaganda created a subversive potential of utopian, oppositional thinking. That tension between ideals and reality, that particular divorce of reason (evidently produced in power relations) from experience, or perhaps the alienation of experience from reason thus constructed, marked the first dimension of schizoid splits in social identity.

Other discrepancies resulted from a particular spatial allocation of value judgments. When assessed in terms of social structure referents, values elicited in the research concerned the self, the "extended self" (objects identified as "mine," first of all family and close friends), the nation, and hardly anything in between. Such a combination of individualism and nationalism (or patriotism, because the only behavior associated with the value of the nation concerned readiness to defend the country in case of military threat) demonstrated a total lack of interest in traditionally defined political issues, a lack of identification with group interests, ideologies, political programs, and social institutions—with anything that is between the closest privacy and the issue of national independence. Such profound alienation from practically all dimensions of social life, described by Nowak as "sociological vacuum," was substituted by a deep integration into molecular family and close peer relations. These identifications were providing both patterns of other social relations and criteria for their examination. One of the results of this phenomenon was the expansion of the "ethics of privacy," which saturated virtually all levels of social structures, both formal and informal. The ethics of privacy was subversive in two aspects: first, it created subject positions opposing "engaged social attitudes" strongly promoted by the media and educational institutions and thus formed a practice of social resistance, of nonparticipation in imposed structures of social life; second, it laid the grounds for enormous corruption, making the state and Communist party bureaucracy virtually impotent. The only visible line of social division was drawn between "us" and "them," "us" including "all like me" and "them" including "those in power" (and nobody really felt in power, and therefore nobody personally belonged to "them"). The "us versus them" structure was a substitute for nonexistent class divisions based on structurally stable and visible criteria (like ownership or kind of work) and was flexible enough to meet the standards of "privacy": a party official who was my acquaintance and could help me in buying scarce goods automatically belonged to "us," not to "them." The socialist culture developed a moral standard of a "good fellow," applicable both to close personal friends and useful, accessible bureaucrats helpful in everyday problems in exchange for bribes or other profits (almost everybody had access to some goods, and almost all goods were scarce and demanded "good fellows" to be obtained). Let us note how flexible the moral standard of a "good fellow" was, how shifting subject positions were being adopted by people who had to enact rituals of "making friends" with representatives of the hated political system, how hybrid and ill defined the identities were of those in middle ranks of power. It seems that these ranks were as numerous as those of the middle class in the West: almost everybody had some power in the process of the constant exchange of services.

The "sociological vacuum" analyzed by Nowak illustrates a phenomenon that Ernesto Laclau characterizes as the "impossibility of society," as a deep ontological rupture that radically challenges the perspectives of establishing social structure. Again, the dramatic outcome of Communist political domination seems to bear some similarity to more general features of the contemporary political situation in the Western world. In Laclau's radical reconstruction of social ontology, the notion of the social is constituted by antagonisms—external, contingent conflicts constantly challenging the constitution of objectivity, of social structure and its identity. Laclau challenges the Hegelian-Marxist notion of dialectical relations taking place within the structure of society or within history, where all conflicts are claimed to be of a necessary, objective nature (like class conflicts resulting from ontologically contradictory interests linked to positions occupied in the structural "base" of the society) and therefore are intrinsic to the process of development. In such interpretations conflicts eventually resolve, and new objective entities appear as a result of synthesizing movement. Objectivity—social structure and social identity—constitutes "itself" in the course of the very process of history. In Laclau's argument this notion of self-constituting objectivity is radically challenged. Antagonisms are of constitutive nature and limit any objectivity attempting to establish itself in the form of identity; they dislocate objectivity and make it contingent. As antagonisms are of external nature, they cannot be resolved in a dialectical manner. All resolutions, and all identities established as a result of them, depend, therefore, on power relations; they have to be imposed. A major part in this process is played by the sphere of myth. Subjects are constructed in language, are mythical and metaphorical subjects, because it is only in myth that the radical contingency of the social can be hegemonized and represented as coherent identity. To put it in the simplest possible way, reality is a flux, is contingent and antagonistic, what makes it coherent and objective, what gives it a shape of identity, is language with its mythical representations. Representation, therefore, does not really "represent" anything external to it, it rather constitutes the objectivity and creates the identity of the social.[11]

In terms of Laclau's position, what Nowak described as the "sociological vacuum" can be understood as a radical rupture in the possibilities of representation, as a lack of objectifying practices of identity formation, that is, as the nonexistence of the social in an ontological sense. Contingent social relations, deprived of an objectifying articulation that gave them the shape of ideological positions, economic interests, and political programs, remained contingent; as a result of Communist rule, society disappeared. It arrived on the historical scene only when the power of the myth was restored with the emergence of the Solidarity movement.[12]

Crucial to Laclau's position, and the element that makes his ideas original among those claiming the nonexistence of society, is radical optimism resulting from such nihilistic premises. His argument is worth quoting at length here:

> We have therefore upheld the contingency of social relations, the ineradicability of power relations, and the impossibility of reaching a harmonious society. . . . Indeed, far from being the cause for pessimism, they are the basis for radical optimism. . . . [I]f social relations are contingent, it means they can be radically transformed through struggle, instead of transformation being conceived as self-transformation of an objective nature; if power is ineradicable, it is because there is radical liberty that is not fettered by any essence; and if opaqueness is constitutive of the social, it is precisely this

which makes access to the truth conceived as an unveiling (*alétheia*) possible. [13]

In spite of some "Leninist aftertaste" a position like this must evoke in my East European memory (it was just the notion of radical transformability of the social that lay the ground for radical political oppression), it presents a fundamental theoretical challenge to postmodern pessimism grounded in the lack of foundations on which to base political and educational projects. The postmodern critique proved to be so successful in dismantling premises of the traditional world order that it left hardly anything behind its sweeping deconstruction. As Frederic Jameson noted in referring to Foucault's theory of power relations, the more powerful such critical analyses are, the more powerless their readers are made; the critical potential of theory is subverted into disempowering paralysis.[14] To draw optimistic conclusions from a deconstructive critique, from the thesis of fundamental dislocation within the structure of society, is of fundamental significance to all social projects. Educational thinking cannot do without such a combination of refined critique and radical hope. This is precisely the combination for which Henry Giroux and Roger Simon argue.[15] Such a critical perspective makes it possible for the discourse of social science, of education and politics, to embrace the postmodern critique as part of a public agenda rather than as an excuse for inaction.

Postmodern theory, then, may become part of educational thinking, as it has in the writings of Henry Giroux, Peter McLaren, and other radical theorists of education in the United States. It may be useful, too, for dealing with phenomena that emerged in Eastern Europe as a result of its socialist experience. But to draw a horizon of common theoretical grounds, we have to pay some attention to differences, to the specificity of educational institutions in the (former) East and the West.[16] This chapter is not a good place for a detailed comparative analysis. Something should be said, however, at least about more general features of the relation between educational institutions and their social and political environment.

This relation is constitutive of power relations that shape educational politics outside and inside the schools, and power relations are, on their part, constitutive of the problem of freedom.

SCHOOL AND DOMINATION: HIDDEN CURRICULA AND POLITICAL CONTROL

In American educational theory the relation between school and the social system has been described in the framework of the sociology of education, particularly in a group of theories stemming from structural-functional analyses of schooling, dealing with the way educational institutions contribute to the reproduction of broader social systems to which they are subordinate. This kind of structural subordination translates itself in a "soft," invisible way into educational practices that take the form of "hidden curricula." There is no visible link between hidden curricula and political institutions; nobody is personally in charge of "hiding" curricula, of making the process of socialization into the status quo invisible and unquestionable. It "just works this way" on a self-regulatory basis of the dynamics of open systems where elements "optimalize" their relations with supersystems. The notion of a hidden curriculum in educational research was a serious blow to the myth of the political innocence of schools, and it inspired critical investigations into the nature of schooling, eventually giving birth to the movement of radical emancipatory pedagogy that fundamentally questioned the whole model of social reproduction as too narrow and one-dimensional.[17]

This model, simplified here, of state-school relations is in one aspect visibly different from the experience of Eastern Europe: schools there, once something like contemporary Eastern Europe emerged, that is, after the Soviet political domination over the region began, were never claimed to be politically innocent. They were never thought to merely serve the need of the "individual development" of the child. It is a bitter paradox that the totally uncritical, idyllic idea of child-centered school appears as an attractive counterdiscourse just now, when the Communist rule has ended, and is gaining some popularity among teachers tired of the notion of the political character of education maintained through-out the Communist domination.

Political and educational doctrines of the region were informed by the Marxist discourse, with its stress on the inevitably ideolog-ical character of all forms of consciousness. This critical insight of Marxism, however, changed its character when it was applied to "constructive politics" rather than to the deconstruction of capital-ism. There is a difference between saying that education is a politically dominated and ideologically informed enterprise in a situation when you criticize the dominant system in order to change it, and in a situation when you use the same argument in order to secure the authority of the dominant political power and to make all claims to freedom sound naive and impotent.

In the 1970s a major educational reform was undertaken in Poland. Calling for the modernization of curricula, it also brought about deep structural changes that made the Polish educational system more compatible with the Soviet one. Similar reforms had been undertaken by other East European countries several years before. Some of the curricular changes, for instance in teaching mathematics, were of a progressive nature, whereas the structural ones had a devastating impact on the quality of education. As some critics pointed out, they were deliberately aimed at depriving whole social groups of developmental opportunities.[18] Education was supposed to perform political functions, to shape the society according to doctrinal goals in such a way that critical interrogation of power relations would be almost impossible, and this function was not hidden in the curricula but was part of the official educa-tional politics of the state. The most direct description of this kind of state-school relation can be found in theoretical studies preced-ing the reform of the 1970s. As social practice is inevitably ideological, argued Heliodor Muszynski, all goals of education must be grounded in *some* ideology.[19] It is, then, within the responsibility of the state to ensure that the goals of education are grounded in the most progressive ideology, serving the needs of the biggest group of people. Using Marxist philosophy, it is easy to prove that it is the ideology of the working class that is the most universal one, the least distorted by interests grounded in the need of securing the status quo, of protecting one's own property and privileges. This progressive ideology is expressed in its best form by the Communist party, which is the avant-garde of the workers' movement, its intellectual background and political tribune. In conclusion, the goals of education should be stated by the party—and so they were.

Adopting progressive, holistic premises of the systems theory, Muszynski developed a theory of educational systems that distinguished between levels of organization and branches of educational activities linked to classified groups of objectives. One of these groups concerned broadly conceived moral education, where the majority of objectives directly linked to the political system belonged, and the realization of these objectives involved, among other measures, strategies based on rituals (like performances, singing, or other kinds of rituals ensuring group identification around "totems," symbols, and so on). Another consequence of this systemic approach was the thesis that subsequent "agents" of school education could differ in their competencies. As long as the party was responsible for stating general aims of education, lower-rank officials (specialists, consultants, counselors) had to be competent in translating these aims into behavioral objectives; teachers, on their part, were to be proficient in techniques of implementation, in educational "know-how," without necessarily asking what they were implementing. All this theoretical argument is an outright process of hiding the curriculum, of translating it into behavioral objectives that are difficult to interrogate and are directly linked to moral issues (like responsibility or identification with the group), and of depriving teachers (to say nothing of the students) of the possibilities of critical understanding. It is funny to think that at the same time when in the United States educators were pondering the question "Who hides the hidden curriculum?" in Poland a renowned scholar did the job and signed it with his name.

This story points to a significant and more general difference in both educational and political systems of the United States and East European socialist countries. What is interesting is that this is not so much a difference in the kind of structural relations between education and politics as it is in the ways of securing the desired shape of these relations. While in the West we can see something like a kind of self-regulatory practice based upon gradual "optimalization" of the relations between supersystems and subsystems, in the East we had a kind of direct hierarchical control of functional parameters of the system. Thus described, these regulations follow the pattern of economic relations, of the free market versus planned, state-controlled distribution of goods. Both these structural models reproduce themselves in everyday operations.

This reconstruction, however, is somehow limited. It is grounded in a structural, systemic analysis implying that there are intrinsic regulatory mechanisms accountable for system development. In one case they can be identified as mechanisms of optimalization, in another as hierarchical control of the supersystem over its subsystems. If this model were adequate, we could expect nothing but evolutionary changes leading toward a state of entropy, of balanced and immobile equilibrium. This way of thinking is being challenged from various positions; the "post-Marxist" and poststructural perspective presented by Laclau is one of them. Basic dislocations I referred to earlier, the antagonistic nature of structural changes, lead to a situation where phenomena are not so much determined as they are overdetermined, exposed to so many various and multidirectional influences that they are virtually contingent, unpredictable, and open to external forces not complying with the logic of the system. The system itself appears to be rather a conceptual or mythical construction than an ontological reality. What this means for the relation between schooling and politics is that there is no one-directional dependency here: schools can serve the status quo as well as they can be subversive to dominant power relations. These relations themselves can be resisted. As numerous analyses conducted in the field of critical pedagogy or the recent history of Eastern Europe clearly show, power relations are actually being challenged on various levels of social life: in classrooms, in social movements, in whole geopolitical regions. Reproduction apparently inscribed into the structure of schooling sometimes just does not work.

Still, in spite of this common feature of dislocation and overdetermination, we have to stress differences between the East and the West in order to avoid the very tempting trap of "sameness," making all explanations easy and restoring, in a postmodern version, good old ontological monism, overinclusive general rules applying in equal proportion to everything. One such visible difference concerns the role of myth in the process of constructing (or deconstructing, revolving, inverting) the social.

It seems that Western societies were to some extent more open to the process of diversified verbalization bringing about some ontological stability to their structures than East European ones. Even if the basic choice they had was limited to two political parties, this meant a possibility of interchanging constitutive myths enabling an occasional change in signifying practices, and therefore—because "representation" is in fact creation of society, as Laclau argues—a change of the society itself. Such a process seems to create a general openness to alternative significations and representations and makes the whole process of constituting the social more open to day-to-day, pragmatic changes. In such a setting the practice of resistance seems to rely on the polyphony of political discourses, on the access to different languages, different categorizations, and different horizons of imagination. Of course, one can argue that these competing signifying practices have more in common than they seem to at first, that they are all modifications, mutations of one and the same foundational myth underlying the whole range of legitimate, *acceptable* political discourses, that differences between accessible political articulations are superficial. This may be true. Superficial differences, however, differences on the surface of reality, are significant; signification itself is a "surface" process. Such differences provide for a variety of subject positions, regardless of how deep they are, how far they reach below the surface. Identification, and thus identities, can be sufficiently based on surfaces.

In the East the political discourse was dominated by one ideology, or rather by a one-dimensional attempt to ideologically hegemonize the fabric of the social. This situation created, on the one hand, a rigid monophony of legitimized politics, and on the other, a vast realm of exclusions with an enormous subversive potential. Practically any ideology except the Communist one was somehow oppositional, external to the system, and dislocated and antagonistic. The whole process of hegemonization depended on one particular articulation, on one myth. This made it extremely vulnerable, and therefore the amount of power demanded to secure this process was enormous. The degree of dependence on power to maintain the social, to prevent it from a slippage into unrecognized nothingness, and not just the monopoly of power itself, made socialism an oppressive, totalitarian system: the threat to its existence was everywhere. Moreover, the process of hegemonization, due to the amount of exclusions, had to result in creating a "false" society, an appearance, something incomprehensible whose structure kept on slipping away from all attempts at representation. These attempts could not bring about the desired shape of the society either. The social remained unknown, unrecognized, dislocated—in a way, nonexistent.[20]

Resistance was easy. It was enough to be Catholic, to own a piece of ground, to read the foreign press, or to tell political jokes to gain an empowering potential of being "against the system." But this accessibility of resistance resulted, as well, in a particular difficulty with identity formation. In the process of identification it is never enough to associate oneself with something; it is equally important to differentiate oneself from something else, to create a sphere of "otherness." As all oppositional discourses were set against one dominant ideology, they all could easily be conceived as basically the same. That lack of differentiation led to the establishment of a dualistic mythical representation (and thus social structure) setting "us" against "them." In that dual structure "they" occupied the first, dominant position. Everyday conversations inevitably oscillated around "them"; people were gaining their identities, establishing communities, and unifying around "them." The very same structure prepared the ground for the revolution of Solidarity. It was enough to reverse the order of domination and subjugation in the mythical structure, to stress "us" instead of "them," to create a powerful social movement integrating all possible, or rather potential, subversive discourses. The way the notion of solidarity was articulated was similar to that of socialism as it was used by the Communist party: it preceded the factual social phenomenon, created it, and projected a state of society. It was a formative myth rather than an expression of popular identities. These had to be formed in the process of differentiation dislocating the movement and bringing it to an end. The introduction of martial law in December 1981 once again reversed the signifying structure, positioned "them" back in the first place, and for some time delayed the process of differentiation, of identification. It was only after the final demise of Communist rule in 1989 that the process of differentiated identity formation brought about the final death of Solidarity and opened up the scary, incomprehensible abyss of politics without cognitive representations, without foundational myths bringing order into the realm of power.

As this exemplary analysis seems to show, the process of reproduction recognized as the basic function of schooling by some critical theorists is entangled in a very complex network of heterogeneous relations that subvert its very nature. Ideological domination creates spheres of exclusions, of "otherness" not incorporated into the system (as the system is being *created*, not just represented, in the process of ideological signification). These exclusions must be kept aside by means of power, but at the same time they create the antagonistic sphere of discourses challenging the very existence of the system. In the West these discourses are dispersed and diversified as long as signifying practices in multi-party systems stress superficial differences as the basis of identity formation. Oppositional movements, forced to articulate their positions on the scene created by dominant discourses, to some extent take over that basic rule of articulation, which pushes them to stress differences between various subversive orientations in order to form their identities and attract public attention (the idea "different is good" is expressed not only by postmodern critical movements but has even become an advertising slogan of Arby's burgers; it circulates around American culture). Monolithic, one-party domination in the East created a situation of unified opposition, of solidarity stressing the "we" embracing everybody who is not "them." This polarized power relation, however, ceases to exist with the demise of the monopoly of legitimate articulation. Solidarity in Poland is over, and the new challenge of diversification is the most urgent one on the political scene. This happens at the same time that oppositional movements in the West have to meet the challenge of solidarity that enables them to form a "rainbow coalition" viable in a political struggle over the definition of reality. Solidarity and difference are, therefore, in play on both sides of the former Iron Curtain; however, they play different roles.[21]

EAST-WEST, RIGHT-LEFT: IDEOLOGICAL GEOGRAPHY AND THE PROBLEM OF EDUCATION

Meanings are located in space. If words can cross borders, meanings are resistant; they tend to linger on, in an inertia calling for past experiences associated with places.

The fall of the Berlin Wall created an apparent openness between East and West. We can communicate, we can hear each other, but this does not mean that we can understand. Understanding takes more than deciphering. Past experiences make it difficult to understand meanings; we keep referring to different realities where they were created. This is not merely a technical problem; it is the problem of our identities.

We tend to remember the wall, the Iron Curtain, as something that separated the East from the West, as an annoying obstacle, as something to be demolished. Then, it was hoped, the world would become one. Military blocs would disappear, economies would merge their resources, and cultures would feed each other with their achievements. We tend to forget that the very same curtain created our identities. To be a "self" requires the presence of the other. The wall was a perfect othering device that physically separated people on both of its sides and thus created referents for cultural identities. Not only, then, did we have to create our identities in separation, we also had to imagine, and virtually create our respective others in order to know who we were.

Robert Young, in his analyses of postcolonial writings, points to an extremely important aspect of identity formation. The process of "othering," of creating one's counteridentity, is not arbitrary; it is grounded in language and therefore follows some structural rules of signification. Jacques Derrida's analyses of language disclose power relations inscribed into this process. Meanings are inevitably paired, organized in binary oppositions, and in each pair the first position is occupied by a dominant concept, a "good" concept, the concept one would like to identify himself or herself with. Structures like "good" and "bad," "male" and "female," "strong" and "weak," and "rational" and "emotional" are employed in the process of identity construction with an obvious tendency to organize one's own image around the "good" side. This leaves the other side for the Other: constructing our identities, we create the sphere of exclusions reserved for "not-me," for somebody different. In this way a cognitive structure is prepared that can be used whenever we actually encounter a stranger; we employ this structure to create the Other. The Other, as Young brilliantly notices in discussing Edward Said's notion of "orientalism," is a creation based on the excluded, repressed, unconscious side of the dominant culture. (As Said disclosed, orientalism originated in the West as the "other" discourse for dealing with non-Western cultures.) Creating the Other, the self displaces and materializes its own unconsciousness, thus creating an image that eventually challenges its own identity.[22] Let us note how challenging indeed to the Western rationalism are the ideas of "other" (Eastern) philosophy, religion, and rationality, ideas derived from the suppressed mysticism of European culture and ascribed solely to the

East; how their presence outside our dominant space makes us aware of our specificity; and how sometimes it forces us to recall our own forgotten "other" rationality.

If we now imagine this kind of process of identity formation with the other physically isolated behind the wall, the wall itself seems to change its image. East and West, as I now see it, were developing their identities constantly facing the wall, as if each was trying to see the other through its concrete slabs. To complete the process, to know who we were, we had to believe that we really did see the other side. When we visualize this process nowadays, however, we can understand that the concrete wall was not transparent, even though it seemed to be so: what we saw was not the Other. East and West saw their mirror reflections, their own reversed reflections. In the mirror, what seems to be ahead is really behind you; what seems to be left is actually right.

Such a reversed perspective results in numerous misunderstandings. Let it suffice to note that progressive social movements on both sides of the wall developed mutually oppositional ideologies: socialism, whatever its form, which is still considered a viable alternative in the Western political system, is oppressive and regressive in the East. Liberal capitalism, market economy, and tough monetary policy, blamed for tremendous social problems in the West, empower people in the East to undertake bold economic and political reforms in the name of a better future and social progress. In recent history we have seen many paradoxes. We have seen Margaret Thatcher supporting Polish workers in their struggle and precisely at the same moment suppressing in a violent way miners' strikes in England. I have heard of Solidarity activists settling down in South Africa after they had fled martial law in Poland and becoming comfortably indifferent to apartheid. We can see progressive reformers in the East eager to follow the most regressive political patterns of the West. Of course, one may argue that this discrepancy in what "progressive" and "reactionary" mean is grounded in structural differences rather than in the issue of identity: economic and political systems on both sides of the Iron Curtain were incompatible; therefore the discourse of change and progress must naturally employ different ideologies, different economic programs and political projects. But if the discrepancy were all about incompatible structures, we would probably face a more diversified scope of mutually isolated alternatives than we can see now. Why is it that the demise of socialism in Eastern Europe resulted in such a severe political crisis in the Western Left? Why are oppositional movements in the West unable to form a program integrating their interests so that they can present it as a viable alternative to the dominant Right's agenda? Why is it that nobody in the East, apart from old Communist party officials, dares to formulate a leftist agenda, even though election results show a significant demand for this kind of political discourse? All these issues, in my opinion, point to a severe crisis of social imagination on both sides of the Iron Curtain, and that crisis can be traced back to the previously discussed question of identity.

In a way we have lost our respective Others. To form our identities anew, we start searching for new aliens and reviving old conflicts. I think that recent increases in racist, ethnic, religious, and other cultural oppression, in violence and intolerance, have to do with this blind and nervous search for otherness. The former bipolar, dualistic structure of references was comfortably "there," ready to use and, in a way, safe. To some extent it erased differences in order to shape a kind of totalized "Western" and "Eastern" identities. But that very structure and that very erasure resulted as well in the crisis of imagination, in an inability to think in utopian terms. To make this more specific, let us consider what happens to an identity formed around the "worse" side of the dualistic structure of oppositions. People in Eastern Europe learned to think about their countries in terms of temporality and provisionality, as something that "cannot last." They knew that theirs was the "worse" economy, culture, and democracy: worse cars, worse fashions, worse drinks, and worse ways of life. Everything that they were experiencing had its ready-to-use better version on the other side of the wall. It was not necessary to imagine; it was enough to emulate, to overcome one's own identity, to displace it to adopt signs of otherness, turning them into the clues of one's desired identity, and to suppress or eliminate all traces of one's "original" identity, turning it into otherness. People living in "worse" cultures, in cultures dominated by icons of other cultures, by idealized images of "the good life" created on the basis of the negation of one's own experience and identified with that "better world behind the wall," develop a readiness for emulation, for a willing subordination of their lives to the signifiers of otherness. This fundamental resistance, the deepest possible resistance to one's own condition, a resistance reaching the very level of cultural identity, paradoxically creates a vulnerability to colonial domination and brings about total alienation and displacement of the self. People locate their affective investments in imported icons of popular culture and develop strong negative feelings toward everything that reminds them of their place. There is a kind of imagination associated with such displacement, but it is a dreamlike imagination of someone who lives his or her life absentmindedly, somewhere else, "in a movie," in a constant hallucination of "being in America." Let us recall Stuart Hall's insight about the postmodern world "dreaming itself to be American."[23] This is the world of those who transferred their eschatological dreams of paradise from time to space, from the future of their own societies—or from the afterlife—to the United States of America or the European Community. Such an orientation destroys political pragmatism. There is no point in improving the life here if the real life is there.

If dreams seem to be the ultimate political reality of those who live in dominated cultures, pragmatism is the privilege of those on the "better" side of the curtain. People in the West tend to believe—through the analogical process of othering, of creating the image of the "worse" life "over there"—that they live in the best of possible worlds, that there is no real viable alternative to their economy and their politics. "They" have tried socialisms, communisms, anarchisms, and all other isms, and they didn't work. What "we" have to do, then, is to improve what can be improved and dismiss what attempts to look beyond the horizon of the present. We are the dream of the world; there is nothing else one could dream about. Such a "proclamation of paradise" is possible only in the situation of physical isolation of the Other from the world of direct experience. It is only through the barriers that we can see ourselves as better than others. Apart from a pragmatic concentration on the minor defects of heavenly life, such a situation produces one more effect in the lives of those who belong to the dominant part of the world, but do not think that they are in heaven. If we are in the best of worlds, and if we are hungry, homeless, oppressed, and poor, what can we do but despair, rage, and reject everything? The difference between pragmatism and despair, freedom and oppression, and wealth and poverty is the "inner wall" mounting within Western societies.

The separation of East and West in their "formative years" created a particular stiffening in the sphere of political imagination. Identities built on the basis of othering, on the lack of dialogical exchange and direct contacts, resulted in the present impossibility of meeting the challenges of a world that does not fall into the simple dualistic structure any longer. We do not understand this world. What was progressive sounds reactionary; the Left is on the Right; our past seems to be a viable project for the future of those whom we meet at the ruins of the wall. Displaced dreaming, small pragmatic improvements, and violent despair do not answer anything. The world we know has fallen apart, has dissolved into local struggles and decentered power relations, and has lost its once clearly visible direction of development. We fear ourselves; we fear the others because for the first time we see that they are like us; we see ourselves in them, and it makes us scared to death, for we do not know who we are any more. There is no border, or everything is the border. We do not know our places in this world. The lack of the Other has made us helpless and vulnerable and has deprived some of us of hope, some of security. Everything has to be renamed. We need new language, new understanding, new imagination, new visions that could re-create the social world.

If the postmodern diagnosis of the contemporary world is convincing, and it seems to be so, education can no longer remain the same. Postmodern and postcolonial discourses taken up by critical pedagogy deal with the challenges I have been referring to.[24] The language of postmodern theory proves effective in discussing issues of subjectivity in a more complex manner than is possible within the premises of traditional modernist assumptions; it makes it possible to take up the question of the construction of the social world in the course of political action, ideological discourses, and cultural representation. Let us note that these issues of subjectivity and society construction are central ones for any pedagogy, especially for one attempting to deal with the whole complexity of the contemporary world. The discourse of postmodernity, however, poses serious questions to pedagogy as well. The previously sufficient grounding of educational ideologies in cultural tradition is no longer possible when the contingent character of the tradition and the political character of the culture have been disclosed; the nature of knowledge, once believed to be the ultimate emancipatory power, proves far more complicated, and it is clear nowadays that knowledge serves the needs of political control at least as well as those of emancipation. The open, contingent character of the social does not make it easier to formulate goals of education, and this difficulty seems to undermine the whole traditional structure of pedagogy as a "hierarchical" discourse of educational practice implementing prescribed objectives. Moreover, the postmodern openness of the social world is understood as the fundamental threat to Western civilization by the conservatives, who reformulate their educational and political agenda around the problems of postmodernity. They keep trying to restore the situation of hegemony, of one-dimensional politics erasing all differences, or—to make things still more complicated—to use the postmodern notion of difference in order to stiffen cultural, economic, and political boundaries around the marginalized groups, enclosing them in numerous ghettolike enclaves of diversity and leaving free and unchallenged ground for the dominant culture and power. This kind of neoapartheid may adopt elements of postmodern discourse, making the distinctions between "Left" and "Right," "progressive" and "conservative" still more complicated. In the age of the demise of European "real socialism," such discursive displacements are far from surprising; this, however, makes the need for their critical interrogation still more urgent.[25] Finally, the discourse of postmodernity, so powerful in disclosing mechanisms of domination, creates serious problems with the notion of freedom. Identity, society, culture, politics—all these spheres present themselves as arenas of struggle, as overwhelmed by domination and control; if anything saves some space for human agency, it seems to be, as Laclau has it, the overdetermination of the human world. This notion, however, does not seem to provide for a satisfactory grounding for the concept of freedom. It may show how some negative freedom, freedom from, is still possible, but it does not say anything about its positive aspects, about freedom to. Definitely the notion of freedom needs some reformulation in the discourse of postmodernity, where all traditional foundations of freedom—like personal autonomy, empowering knowledge, reason as the source of ultimate control over nature and society, science as the instrument of unlimited progress, the cultural superiority of the West and its democratic institutions—have been wiped away in a sweeping deconstruction of the Western cultural heritage.

Emancipatory pedagogy embracing the discourse of postmodernity seems to be able to deal with most complex problems of the contemporary world, but it is at the same time challenged on its own ground in two ways. First, it is challenged on the issue of the possibilities of grounding the project of education in a world where there are no clear directions, where old political and ideological maps have ceased to show ways anywhere. Second, it is challenged in the project of emancipation in a world that has undermined the meaning of freedom and so far has not provided us with clear clues what this notion could mean. The following chapters are an attempt to discuss these problems.

NOTES

1. Uri L. Zagumenov, "In the High Hope of Cooperation" (Paper delivered at the University Council for Educational Administration Annual Conference, Baltimore, Maryland, 1991).

2. Henry A. Giroux, "Educational Leadership and the Crisis of Democratic Culture" (Address delivered at the University Council for Educational Administration Annual Conference, Baltimore, Maryland, 1991).

3. See, for instance, Steven Connor, *Postmodernist Culture: An Introduction to Theories of the Contemporary* (New York: Basil Blackwell, 1989); Roy Boyne and Ali Rattansi, eds., *Postmodernism and Society* (New York: St. Martin's Press, 1990); Ihab Hassan, *Paracriticisms: Seven Speculations of the Times* (Urbana: University of Illinois Press, 1975); Andrew Ross, ed., *Universal Abandon? The Politics of Postmodernism* (Minneapolis: University of Minnesota Press, 1988); Madan Sarup, *An Introductory Guide to Post-structuralism and Postmodernism* (Athens: University of Georgia Press, 1989). On educational analyses of postmodernity, see Stanley Aronowitz and Henry A. Giroux, *Postmodern Education: Politics, Culture, and Social Criticism* (Minneapolis: University of Minnesota Press, 1991); Henry A. Giroux, ed., *Postmodernism, Feminism, and Cultural Politics: Redrawing Educational Boundaries* (Albany: State University of New York Press, 1991).

4. I am referring to the notion of "simulacrum" proposed by J. Baudrillard, widely used in postmodern writings. See, for example, an analysis in Linda Hutcheon, *The Politics of Postmodernism* (London and New York: Routledge, 1989), pp. 11, 33–34.

5. This reconstruction of selected aspects of Jacques Derrida's philosophy is based on the following texts by him: "The End of Book and the Beginning of Writing," in *Of Grammatology*, trans. Gayatri Ch. Spivak (Baltimore: Johns Hopkins University Press, 1976); "Implications: Interview with Henri Ronse," in *Positions*, trans. Alan Bass (Chicago: University of Chicago Press, 1981); "Différance," in *Margins of Philosophy*, trans. Alan Bass (Chicago: University of Chicago Press, 1982); and "Deconstruction and the Other," in Richard Kearney, *Dialogues with Contemporary Continental Thinkers: The Phenomenological Heritage* (Manchester, England: Manchester University Press, 1984).

6. See Michel Foucault, *Power/Knowledge: Selected Interviews and Other Writings, 1972–1977* (New York: Pantheon Books, 1980).

7. See L. H. Martin, H. Gutman, and P. H. Hutton, eds., *Technologies of the Self: A Seminar with Michel Foucault* (Amherst: University of Massachusetts Press, 1988). The notion of subjectivity proposed by Foucault in these texts is in a way different from the one developed in

his analyses of power: it is less deterministic, and it takes into account the process of self-construction of subjectivity. I will refer to these concepts later on, when I discuss the problem of identity construction in relation to power (see chapter 2). Foucault's analyses of power, with their claims that deprive individuals of developmental autonomy, are more characteristic and were more influential in the discourse of postmodernity, and therefore I will concentrate on them in this part of the presentation.

8. Frederic Jameson, "Postmodernism, or the Cultural Logic of Late Capitalism," *New Left Review*, no. 146 (July–August 1984), pp. 53–92.

9. I am using this term after Stuart Hall. See Stuart Hall, "The Meaning of New Times," in Stuart Hall and Martin Jacques, eds., *New Times: The Changing Face of Politics in the 1990s* (London: Verso, 1990).

10. Stefan Nowak, "System wartosci spoleczenstwa polskiego," *Studia Socjologiczne*, no. 4 (1979): 155–173.

11. Ernesto Laclau, *New Reflections on the Revolution of Our Time* (London: Verso, 1990), pp. 5–12, 17–22, 31–33, 89–93.

12. It is interesting to note that interpretations similar to Laclau's appeared in Polish social theories dealing with the nature of socialism and with the Solidarity revolution. Jadwiga Staniszkis was writing about the mythological nature of the movement and about the necessity of mythological identifications when "structural" identities (like classes) had been destroyed during the Communist restructurization of the state; eventually she identified the ontological nature of socialism as "appearance," as "false being" established in the course of forceful implementation of doctrinal premises. Her writings, however, unlike Laclau's, draw heavily on Hegel. Perhaps such grounding is more than justified. Socialist societies were, in a way, purposefully constructed in a "top-down" manner, and therefore they bore more features of systemic, cognitive coherence than capitalist ones. That coherence, however, was accessible only on the level of ideology. Identity preceded society; it was grounded in ideas prior to its (non)existence. Therefore it in a way implanted its own dislocation into the structure of society, making it virtually incomprehensible, contingent, and unrecognized. See Jadwiga Staniszkis, "Wlasnosc, racjonalnosc, dynamika, struktura," *Przeglad Polityczny*, no. 4 (1984): pp. 21–34; "Ontologia realnego socjalizmu (pierwsze przyblizenie)," *Krytyka*, no. 26 (1987): pp. 56–68.

Once again I would like to stress the similarity of outcomes of apparently isolated political processes in the West and the East. In both cases society is eventually identified as "impossible," as something to be established through the constant practice of mythological representation and critique; see the discussion on the democratic possibilities of "contingent" societies in Laclau, in this chapter.

13. Laclau, *New Reflections on the Revolution of Our Time*, pp. 35–36.

14. Jameson, "Postmodernism, on the Cultural Logic of Late Capitalism," p.57.

15. See Roger Simon, "For a Pedagogy of Possibility," *Critical Pedagogy Networker* 1, no. 1 (1988): pp. 1–4; Henry A. Giroux and Roger Simon, "Popular Culture and Critical Pedagogy: Everyday Life as a Basis for Curriculum Knowledge," in Henry A. Giroux and Peter McLaren, eds., *Critical Pedagogy, the State, and Cultural Struggle* (Albany: State University of New York Press, 1989), pp. 236–252.

16. I have serious problems with referring to "my" part of Europe. It has become a particular vacuum, a nonexisting society in a way, in Laclau's meaning of this notion, something without objectivity, without identity, deprived of constitutive mythology. We were "East" in terms of rigid military divisions and political systems setting us against the "West." Nowadays, however, I have a feeling that in using the term "East" in relation to the region that is becoming "westernized" (sometimes in a really "wild West" manner), I am not doing justice to Asia, to cultures fighting for their cultural identities against Western colonial and neo-colonial domination. Eastern Europe is not a "West," either, however much people there would want it to be. A hybrid, a nowhere, a between? A break between colonizations: after the Soviet, just before some Western one? If I am using the term "East" in relation to Poland and other countries of the region, I am doing so in order to say "a not-yet-West," another Europe, a Europe becoming dependent on "the" Europe and "the" West.

17. For critiques of theories of reproduction, see Henry A. Giroux, *Theory and Resistance in Education* (South Hadley, Mass.: Bergin and Garvey, 1983), pp. 98–107; and "Theories of Reproduction and Resistance in the New Sociology of Education," *Harvard Educational Review* 53, no. 3 (1983): 282–293.

18. According to Zbigniew Kwiecinski, structural reform in rural areas, replacing small local schools with huge bureaucratic institutions

where children were obligatorily bused, was aimed at creating a social infrastructure that would destroy strong local communities that were difficult to manage by political administration, and thus at preparing the ground for Soviet-style collectivization of farmland. (Polish peasants managed to keep private ownership of land during the Communist rule). See Zbigniew Kwiecinski, *Koniecznosc, niepokoj, nadzieja: Problemy oswiaty w latach 70–tych* (Warszawa: Wydawnictwo LSW, 1982), pp. 229–230.

19. See Heliodor Muszynski, *Ideal i cele wychowania* (Warszawa: PZWS, 1972).

20. As I mentioned in note 12, this process of creating the sphere of appearances "instead" of society in socialism was superbly described by Jadwiga Staniszkis.

21. Political events in Poland during June and July 1992—the breakdown of Jan Olszewski's government, the row over former secret police files, attempts to create a broad coalition government based on political parties with programs as discrepant as possible—seem to show some swing of the pendulum in the dynamics of solidarity and difference. Most probably, the process of differentiation has reached the limits of peaceful coexistence, and the challenge of solidarity is present once again. This time, however, at stake is a more difficult kind of solidarity than the one experienced during the revolutionary 1980s: solidarity without a single enemy, solidarity without a solid ground.

22. Robert Young, *White Mythologies: Writing History and the West* (London: Routledge, 1990), pp. 139–140.

23. "Postmodernism . . . is about how the world dreams itself to be 'American.' " Stuart Hall, quoted in Andrew Ross, "Introduction," in Andrew Ross, ed., *Universal Abandon? The Politics of Postmodernism* (Minneapolis: University of Minnesota Press, 1988), p. XII.

24. See especially Aronowitz and Giroux, *Postmodern Education*; Giroux, ed., *Postmodernism, Feminism, and Cultural Politics*; Henry A. Giroux, *Border Crossings: Cultural Workers and the Politics of Education* (New York: Routledge, 1992). In a more detailed way the issues of postmodern education will be discussed in chapters 2 and 3.

25. This peculiar phenomenon of deterritorialization of ideological positions has also been documented by leading representatives of the American Right. Allan Bloom, who identifies many aspects of the postmodern situation and "blames" American cultural ignorance on them, notes, for example, that the philosophy of Friedrich Nietzsche,

once located on the political Right, is today used as an important source of inspiration by the Left. However, instead of concluding that something has changed in the ways political discourses are nowadays positioned one against another, Bloom calls for a retreat to "original sources" of meanings and formulates an educational agenda based upon "Great Books" of the (European) past. Perhaps, as a European, I should be satisfied; but I do not understand, besides my resistance to such attempts at restoring canonical education that erases cultural differences, how one can possibly draw the "bottom line" of the meaning of cultural phenomena. Following Bloom's suggestion, we will inevitably end up with the idea that only the first word ever said was authentic, original, and ultimately true; the rest is cultural distortion, Nietzsche and all Great Books included. This, by the way, is an idea close to some fundamentalist Christian movements. The problem with this perspective is that it seems to rely on a totally temporal way of understanding culture, overlooking the present, the spatial, as the domain of meaning. Bloom's fascination with the European past can explain his partial position, but definitely cannot justify it as an educational project. By erasing the present, we erase practical, ethical responsibility, which can hardly be considered an educational attitude. See Allan Bloom, *The Closing of the American Mind: How Higher Education Has Failed Democracy and Impoverished the Souls of Today's Students* (New York: Simon and Schuster, 1987).

Chapter Two

The Eye, the Tongue, and the Self: Power, Identity, and the Problem of Freedom

The problem of postmodern emancipatory education, when I first started to investigate it, seemed to be based on a paradox. The idea of emancipation somehow implies a notion of freedom and of a free human subject, if not as a condition, then as an outcome of emancipatory endeavors. Both these notions are hardly present in the discourse of postmodernism, apart from appearing as objects of deconstruction. The fruitful encounter of critical social sciences with the thought of postmodernity proves, therefore, disquieting at the same time. The conceptual framework of postmodernism is effective in discovering and deconstructing subsequent layers of human dependency and enslavement in the critique of how human beings are conditioned and constructed in dissolved power relations permeating the fabric of personal and social life. However, powerful as it is as a discourse of deconstruction, the language of postmodernism seems to be difficult to use in thinking in terms of freedom. Also postmodern theory seems rather hostile to the notion of subjectivity. Without concepts of freedom and subjectivity, the notion of emancipation is hard to explain.

Is there a possibility of formulating an idea of freedom within the postmodern? If so, the freedom of whom or of what, considering the often declared death of the subject? To make these questions even more complicated, the postmodern theory of education is far from being coherent. I would rather say that there are various educational reactions to postmodernity, some of which gain more importance than others due to their theoretical self-consciousness and their serious attempts to critically position themselves within, or in relation to, postmodern theoretical discourses. I will not be able to discuss all of them. I will rather try to draw a conceptual map of some of the most significant, in my opinion, postmodern pedagogies, with a particular purpose in mind: to draw the boundaries of the postmodern question of freedom.

The analysis will have to tackle the notion of power as one of the most significant concepts of postmodern social sciences, on the one hand, and as the concept that is oppositional to the notion of freedom, on the other. Although postmodern theories hardly deal with freedom, it seems to me that consideration of their refined and precise analyses of the notion of power may result in a similarly refined reformulation of the notion of freedom. The analysis will have to deal with the notion of subjectivity and how it is constructed in power relations, and hence in what way, if at all, it is free. The question here is whether there is a way of gaining (or preserving) personal and collective autonomy in such relations, and what the role of education is in this process. I will try to propose a very general theoretical grounding for educational analyses of freedom rather than present particular pedagogies in their whole complexity. This analysis will mostly serve the need of constructing a broader conceptual map and will mark exemplary positions on its surface; it will not be an accurate monograph of postmodern pedagogies.

To begin with, I would like to concentrate for a while on an "educational history of freedom." This will be a brief, idealized account of the background of the contemporary problem of emancipation through education.

EDUCATIONAL HISTORY OF FREEDOM: KNOWLEDGE, ENLIGHTENMENT, LIBERATION

Knowledge, and particularly rational knowledge, has a special place in the history of freedom. As Isaiah Berlin put it:

> From Zeno to Spinoza, from the Gnostics to Leibnitz, from Thomas Hobbes to Lenin and Freud, the battle-cry has been essentially the same; the object of knowledge and the methods of discovery have often been violently opposed, but that reality is knowable, and that knowledge and only knowledge liberates, and absolute knowledge liberates absolutely—that is common to many doctrines which are so valuable a part of Western civilization.[1]

Knowledge and freedom are inevitably linked to education. Beginning with Plato, through the Stoics, to the contemporary, with a particular place reserved for the Enlightenment, Reason was considered as the basis of freedom, and education was conceived as a way of liberation. In every case Reason has had a literally critical part to play, has had to provide distance from "first layers" of cognitive experiences, from shadows of reality, whose easily accessible picture is always blurred, be it by illusions and contingency of sensual perceptions, by ideological manipulations performed by the mighty who substitute rituals of faith for clear ideas, or by illusions of certainty resulting from ignorance concerning the nature of cognition. The relation between reason and the practice of enlightenment (making clear or lucid, clarifying) establishes the practice of "leading to the light," drawing out of darkness, out of the cave—the practice of liberation. Reason, freedom, and education have the same mythological root in the idea of light.

In contemporary education we can see some loosening of this relation, taking place simultaneously in several ways, although the basic presumption concerning the links between reason (recently knowledge, which is a broader concept), freedom (more often nowadays referred to as democracy), and education is still maintained. Maxine Greene writes about the relation between critical thinking, articulation of one's voice, and public spheres crucial to creating democratic social relations.[2] Henry Giroux stresses in his numerous texts the role of knowledge in questioning and interrogating the perspective of experience in emancipatory education.[3] Roger Simon writes: "I think that the project of possibility requires an education rooted in a view of human freedom as the understanding of necessity and transformation of necessity."[4] In all these propositions of contemporary critical pedagogy we can see some traces of the tradition of the Enlightenment, as well as of some Marxist activism congruent with that tradition.

The long-lasting discussion between positive and negative ideas of freedom is apparently not taken up in the discourse of critical pedagogy. Positive freedom (freedom to) and negative freedom (freedom from) are treated in contemporary pedagogies of liberation in their mutual interrelatedness. This is visible in a twofold conceptualization of liberating practices. On the one hand, there is a notion of "emancipation," which is clearly "negative" (emancipation presupposes a force from which one is to be liberated); on the other, we have the notion of "empowerment," which stresses positive aspects of freedom. Such a twofold formulation seems to result from a history of emancipatory thinking in education, from the revision of its classical, liberal assumptions.

Liberation presupposes some limits that have to be overcome. The first conceivable sphere of human limitations is set up by the natural world, and educational liberation requires competencies to control this world, that is, to understand the rules of nature and to be able to convert them into technological rules making people qualified to subordinate natural processes to human needs. Of course, natural knowledge and the natural sciences play the most important role in such educational empowerment. Francis Bacon's "Knowledge is power" referred to this sphere of control. This notion of pedagogical liberation seems to reach its climax in the positivist cognitive and didactic doctrine. The encyclopedic knowledge of natural phenomena was supposed to question the ideological domination of the Church and to free societies from its authoritarian domination, to open up a way for rational organization of social life implementing the ideals of freedom, equity, and justice. In positivism this "naturalistic" strategy of control started to include control over social phenomena, as the method of science was used to create the body of scientific social knowledge.

This form of positivism was continued in a particular way by the socialist pedagogy in the Soviet Union and East European countries. In the Communist mythology, which was built on the notion of scientific control over history ("scientific socialism"), the power of humanity was also measured against natural forces. The proverbial ability to reverse the direction of rivers (which brought about quite real ecological disasters in the USSR) was used to demonstrate the infinite human possibilities of the people living in the fully human, socialist state, and thus to legitimize the oppressive political system of that state. The major concern of that scientistic pedagogy was to provide a systematic scope of scientific knowledge, mostly concerning natural phenomena, to transmit the scientistic idea of knowledge (that is, that only scientific knowledge is legitimate), and thus to exclude the sphere of cultural and individual experiences not controlled by the method of science.

The positivist approach to knowledge, reducing legitimate cognition to the sphere of science, had an impact on Western pedagogy as well. Here, however, scientism was associated not so much with the idea of rational control over history as with the notion of individual competitiveness and the free play of natural, political, and economic forces bringing about progress, conceived as a growing capacity of adjustment. These are naturalistic ideas, derived directly from Darwinism, and they have their prominent place in the history of positivism. In political philosophy they are expressed in the form of classical liberalism, in the notion of society being created by free individuals in the course of their competing actions oriented toward individually profitable ends. This kind of liberal attitude brings about two major educational consequences: the direct one, the postulate of freeing individual students from any form of coercion and constraints (for example,

Rousseau), and the indirect, curricula preparing the young for free choices in the future. In some articulations these two notions are unified in the form of projects of educating for (future) freedom through (present) free choices. Carl Rogers's pedagogical ideas are a good example of this approach.[5]

Liberal pedagogy in its "humanistic" articulation (like the Rogersian one) features some notions absent from the classical positivist approach and even contradictory to its basic assumptions. They result from discoveries concerning "new" spheres of human limitations, this time related to the limits of reason itself. This is an outcome of the appropriation of the psychoanalytic critique of rationality. If human behavior is not fully rational, and if we are to be free—to be "fully functioning, self-actualizing personalities," to use Rogers's terminology—we have to learn how to communicate with our repressed, unconscious side. Freedom to learn, learning in a facilitating, nonoppressive environment, is supposed to eliminate repression and free individuals from uncontrolled, unconscious factors shaped by interiorized external domination.

To some extent the experience of liberal pedagogy, particularly its negative experience, demonstrating the weakness and vulnerability of such a theoretical position, can be considered to be a contributing factor to the broadening of the scope of emancipatory discourse in education. Radically critical pedagogy took into account the experience of liberal educators and claimed that it is not merely authoritarian individuals who oppress the young in schools. The main factor underlying oppression in schools is the political character of education, the relation between schools and broader social systems. If people are to be made free, educational interests must focus on that functional relation between school and society. Here we have theories of economic, cultural, and political reproduction, as well as theories of resistance against such domination.[6] At first, educational analyses seemed to focus on centralized, systemic structures (like capital or dominant culture), and theories made use of Marxist, structural, and functional approaches. Further analyses, however, show a set of discontinuities in the process of reproduction and turn to other languages. This proves that limitations of freedom are grounded not merely in hierarchical structures in relation to which individuals play roles of subordinate elements; they are inherent in diluted, decentered, and almost invisible structures that are internalized in the very process of identity formation—in the language, emotions, and desires; in the constitution of the body; and in the grammar of all communicative actions, like advertising, popular culture, mass-media images, and so on. Individuals thus become agents of their own enslavement, and to some extent this is an inevitable process, as their subjectivities, as Foucault shows, are constructed in the process of subjection.[7]

In such a theoretical postmodern, poststructural perspective, it is very difficult to maintain a traditional, liberal notion of freedom. If freedom were to retain its liberal image, if it were still to be understood as freedom from, the process of liberation would have to mean liberating people from themselves, from their own subjectivities, as this is where subjection is inscribed. As Michel Foucault puts it, subjectivities, as well as knowledge and reason, are produced in the course of power relations. It is reason and knowledge that carry on the relations of domination and subjection. Emancipatory claims of reason are, then, quite paradoxical. As Foucault once put it, "A reason . . . can have an effect on emancipation on condition that it manages to liberate itself from itself."[8] How, then, can it be liberating?

POSTMODERN FREEDOM

This sketchy reconstruction of the discourse of liberation in education does not have a chronological character. It attempts to show merely a part of the genealogy of contemporary problems of emancipatory education. These problems are staged not so much in time as they are in space, on the surface of the contemporary, which serves as a screen on which past tendencies and theoretical articulations are projected. The postmodern situation leads to revisions and new articulations of past theoretical standings, positions them in different relations, and forces them to play out their differences one against another in a new discourse of freedom. None of the past tropes of this discussion have vanished; they are all present and stand one next to another, though they are deprived of their clear historical identity. The notion of freeing people from nature recurs today in struggles over sexuality, euthanasia, gender roles, race, and abortion. Nature has become today a cultural construct like all other factors concerning our lives. Liberation from nature means both gaining control over one's body (and here trivial issues like "keep-fit" ideology stand next to such questions as abortion or euthanasia) and freeing ourselves from the cultural notion of nature, demystifying the "naturality" of racial differences, gender roles, and sexual orientations. Let us notice how, in another site of articulations, the idea of the liberating power of natural sciences recurs in the conservative discourse of educational politics in the United States, where it is employed as a magical prescription for economic recession. What is at stake now, however, is not the issue of freeing people from "blind forces of Nature" or of using these forces to increase human capacities, but the problem of creating technologies and management techniques that secure domination over the world, threatened by Japanese and European competition. Such a combination of scientism and global politics is clearly visible in *America 2000*. At the same time these discourses can employ, for instance, the liberal concept of freedom of choice, apparently mixing all possible traditions of emancipatory politics.

In such a situation the traditional approach to the investigation of freedom (like analyzing its concept, discussing relations between "freedom" and "liberty," distinguishing between kinds of freedom, and so on) sounds irrelevant and futile. What we need is rather an analysis of the dynamics of freedom, of "freedom in action," in conflicts, in social practices, in the process of identity formation, and in relation to power. Neither historical nor analytical approaches seem to address the postmodern, spatial, horizontal scene of philosophy; philosophy today seems rather to be enacted than written and read. If, however, one insists on trying to write about freedom, one should write about the social. This is where freedom, if it is discussed at all, is argued about and defined, and where it potentially resides. The dynamics of freedom have to be grasped in the context of power relations, of subjection, resistance, individual and collective identities, society, and politics. Politics, then, is at the beginning (power, domination) and at the end (society, politics, the question of democracy) of this chain of relations. Politics draws the horizon of the discourse of freedom. The question of identity, despite all poststructural deconstructions, appears to be in the middle of that horizon. All that set of relations precisely matches the area of the discourse of critical, radical pedagogy, where the possibilities and responsibilities of educational interventions within this horizon are discussed and argued about.

The analysis of the problem of freedom I am going to undertake will take the notion of the sociogenesis of freedom as the point of departure. This notion was elaborated by Zygmunt Bauman.[9] I will try to broaden the scope of Bauman's investigations and relate the issue of freedom more directly to the problem of identity formation—which, after all, is what education is about. Then I will proceed to the analysis of some educational theories that relate to the postmodern definition of the contemporary world. What I hope to achieve is a generally oriented "map" of educational thinking concerned more or less directly with the problem of freedom in postmodernity.

The fundamental thesis of Bauman's analysis is that individual freedom, as well as the free individual, is a historical construct, and that freedom is a social relation. Freedom always relates to a state of not being free. Whenever in history some social subject was proclaimed free, it was so in opposition to other subjects who were deprived of freedom. Freedom has always been a privilege, says Bauman. A paradigmatic model of the relation of freedom, adopted in Bauman's analysis, is that of Jeremy Bentham's *Panopticon*, an ideal institution of control, considered as typical of contemporary power relations by Michel Foucault. People who work as supervisors and monitor the behavior of the inhabitants of

Panopticon are free in relation to their subjects, being not free at the same time in relation to the central supervisor, the owner, the entrepreneur who can watch their work without being seen by them. Uneven access to knowledge is the crucial element in this relation of freedom and control. Individuals, who do not know whether they are observed at a given moment, behave as if they were observed continuously and thus interiorize the mechanism of control. Visual control, gaze, and knowledge, or rather distribution of "un-knowledge," present major factors of power in this model of social relations.

Individual freedom (which is "just freedom" in the eyes of the contemporary) is not a creation of recent history; it has been known for ages. However, it was always considered to be a goal for those who pursued spiritual values, for saints, eremites, and the like, and it is only recently that this kind of freedom has gained the dominant position and become a model of freedom for all. It is only in capitalism that individual freedom became a social standard. In the background of this phenomenon is the decline of feudal political and normative structures, the radical decentralization of power in early capitalism. For the first time people became subject to many, instead of one, and often conflicting sources of power. This situation raised the question of individual choice and individual responsibility. In capitalism people have been forced to choose their political allegiances, and made responsible for these choices. This basic uncertainty, resulting from the demise of monocentric power, is in the background of the modern notion of freedom. But also in capitalism freedom is relational and implies that somebody is not free. On the global scale, capitalist democracies were constructed on the basis of political and economic domination over non-European colonies (this issue is not discussed by Bauman, however; it is one of the basic assumptions of postcolonial theory, and I will refer to it later on). On the smaller, "inner" scale, individual freedom is contrasted, as Bauman puts it, to the overwhelming instrumentality of social relations, being also a product of capitalism. With the decentration of power there appeared a new dimension of oppression, a new way of not being free—social oppression experienced as the invisible, impersonal power of the "system." As a remedy, a kind of "secondary" freedom is being sought, a freedom from this kind of social control. People start to seek privacy, to try to hide before "the eye of power" behind the thick walls of the bourgeois home.

The capitalist freedom of choice at first realized itself in the domain of economics as a possibility of deciding on where to allocate one's assets (money, labor, resources, and so on). But this is no longer so. What is characteristic of contemporary Western societies is the extremely high concentration of capital, and practically no individual has a chance to challenge huge corporations in economic competition. Instead, contemporary capitalism provides for another kind of freedom. Individual freedom of economic activities, associated with the ethics of work, with identities based upon professional roles, has been replaced by individual freedom of consumption, and along with it by a totally new situation of identity formation, and generally by a new political situation. This change was gradual, and progressive workers' movements had a share in it. Trade unions, struggling for access to political power related to industrial production, achieved something else instead: wage increases, and with them some hope for a better standard of living. In a piecemeal way a new political mechanism was thus created, where property and power ceased to be questioned, and freedom of choice was "tracked" into the consumer's market. This mechanism proved viable and safe for the system; for the first time in history a kind of freedom was invented that was not threatening to the political system and its power relations. On the contrary, consumers' choice was made crucial to its maintenance. Individual competition on the buyer's market does not concern any kind of limited resources, as it is all about symbols, and symbols can be produced without restrictions. Buying anything, a consumer buys a sign of prestige, a mark of social status. Abundance of available goods creates enormous possibilities of individualizing one's own image, of creating a unique style, of expressing most idiosyncratic attitudes and beliefs. To create one's individual image became a virtue, the purchase of symbols, of goods bearing symbolic meaning, became a moral obligation, an act of supporting the society whose economy is based on consumption. Let us note that a factor of the state of the economy most carefully watched and systematically reported by the media, consumers' confidence, is based upon an ethical concept: the moral category of confidence was translated into an index of buyers' attitudes to goods and money. Thus ethics started to concern particular behavior in shopping malls.

One of the elements of this description of freedom relations will play a crucial role in the later part of this presentation, the idea of expressing one's individuality through the purchase of goods bearing visible signs of status (actually, the purchase of anything). As Bauman writes, "The self becomes identical with visual clues other people can see and recognize as meaning whatever they are intended to mean."[10] Thus the construction of subjectivity is based on purchase, and so is the feeling of security, which is one of the major features of a defined identity. (Later on, I will refer to the visual aspect of this process.) In this situation, as Bauman puts it, the main mechanism of power consists in seduction, in drawing people into the market and making them buy things in order to reach the state of security and clear-cut identity. Advertising, along with the whole range of "politics of representation," becomes a crucial mechanism of social control.

This kind of freedom, like any other, implies some kind of not being free. In this case it is poverty. Lack of financial resources results in inability to make decisions based on freedom of choice. The poor are confined to welfare institutions, and these inevitably mark their clients with stigmatizing signs of dependency, of inferiority in the hierarchy of social beings (a particular place of living, special health-care facilities, food supplies, donated clothing, and so on). These signs are clearly distinct, visibly different from those of freedom, and they serve the double role of a background for those who do not have to depend on welfare institutions and of a deterrent against "sinking" into dependence. Poverty is a stigma of exclusion, a mark of being unable to live up to the consumer's ethos—that is, to spend the money. The stigmatized fall into the state of social isolation and self-isolation; they cease to exist as citizens. "In a society of free consumers," says Bauman, "being told by the authorities how to spend one's money is a source of shame."[11]

It seems obvious that freedom of consumption, in spite of its significant feature of making individually created personal images the base of social identities, is not the freedom fought for by critical theorists of emancipatory education. What is at stake is some other kind of freedom; emancipatory endeavors must be grounded in a nonexisting, utopian space reaching outside the experience of real societies and beyond visible alternatives to their notions of freedom. These alternatives are limited by their confinement to the status quo; they are the "other side" of what is known from everyday political experience. The division between East and West served very well the function of providing for such a mutually limited discourse of freedom in Euro-American culture. In the propaganda of the West, freedom of consumption was contrasted with bureaucratic communism. Communism was presented as an extrapolation of the image of welfare institutions to the whole political and economic system. In such a comparison it was evidently better to choose than to be chosen for, to create one's own image than to wear dull, uniform clothes deprived of any personal features. The point is, however, that such an alternative is an ideological closure, a kind of mystification. As Bauman says:

> The strength of the consumer-based social system, its remarkable capacity to command support or at least to incapacitate dissent, is solidly grounded in its success in denigrating, marginalizing or rendering invisible all alternatives to itself except blatant bureaucratic domination. It is this success that makes the consumer incarnation of freedom so powerful and effective—and so invulnerable.[12]

That third, hidden, suppressed alternative Bauman refers to, and critical pedagogy seems to be oriented toward, is "individual autonomy pursued through communal cooperation and grounded in communal self-rule."[13] Due to the "mirror effect" of East-West relations, the same false alternative, making the same third way invisible, was effectively employed by Communist propaganda. In socialist states equity (well, yes, bureaucratic—but how to achieve it otherwise?) and economic justice (well, poor—but as soon as we pay the debts, complete the process of building the "heavy" foundations of industry, develop the consumer-goods production sector, and so on) were presented as having, as the only alternative, injustice, insecurity, and the stupefying superficiality of consumerist capitalism. In such a context the freedom searched for in the discourse of critical pedagogy is neither "Left" nor "Right": it challenges the whole political system based on the division between consumerist capitalism and bureaucratic socialism.

In my opinion, Zygmunt Bauman's *Freedom* presents an outstanding and inspirational analysis of the structural dynamics of freedom, showing its relations to decentered structures of power, to mechanisms of identity formation, to new forms of oppression produced in corporate capitalism, and to some ways of coping with them (like hiding before the gaze in privacy). These elements create a powerful structure that I will try to employ, with some modifications, in my further analysis. It seems to me that Bauman has made only a partial use of this structure, and that its significance extends the aspects of contemporary relations of freedom that he presented in his book. Elements of this structure were used by Bauman to describe the power of gaze and the process of constructing identity on the basis of visual clues. They were not used to analyze other dimensions of power, such as knowledge, and it seems that the same method of analysis could prove fruitful in analyzing a far broader scope of aspects related to freedom relations. Apart from knowledge, which I have mentioned, there are other dimensions of power disclosed in writings of Michel Foucault and other contemporary thinkers.

As the distribution of knowledge constructs subjectivities, so does the politics of the body, "biopolitics" constructing the "body/subject."[14] Foucault grounds this mechanism of control first of all in mechanisms of surveillance developed in order to deal with juvenile sexuality, then extended to control the whole sphere of affects, desires, and privacy. Power is conceived here as a productive, not just a restricting, force, as a factor constituting personal identities. Biopower stems from the interest of the state in "public health," in the condition of the biological population, of the "living resources" of the state. Control over sexuality, health politics, and welfare are all results of the right of the state to intervene into the sphere of the body of individuals (nutrition, procreation, hygiene, and so on). This politics is supported by politics of representation, in particular by textualization of the body, at first repressing its sexuality and thus turning it into the object of desire, then using needs thus created to manipulate behavior (for example, in advertising). The body plays a major role in popular culture and is a major referent and addressee of its messages.[15] These are all elements of the politics whose major concern is the "reason of the state," the well-being of the state with all its resources (the human population included). Modern states claim their rights to decide on the issues of biological life and death of their citizens. As Foucault notes, the politics of public hygiene, of nationalized welfare and health services, appears on the scene of history just at the time of the first national wars, which engaged whole populations and demanded certain duties on the part of everybody inhabiting a given territory. When the state starts claiming its rights to people's lives, it takes up the care of their health as well.

Language is still another dimension of contemporary power, strictly connected with the issue of knowledge. Poststructural linguistics makes the language open to the sphere of politics. As Derrida points out, dualistic categorizations within the language are never "innocent"; they bear certain valuations usually ascribing positive value to the first concept in every pair of categories. Robert Scholes has made an extensive use of this idea in his project of education for "textual power" (I will refer to this project in chapter 3).[16] In other analyses the relation between the language and the unconscious is stressed. These interpretations usually employ Lacan's linguistic reinterpretation of psychoanalysis[17] and contribute to our understanding of how subjectivities and identities are constructed through the impact of language—or, just like linguistic phenomena, within language, within the process of representations, as Stuart Hall puts it.[18] Postcolonial theorists point to a very particular and meaningful aspect of the linguistic construction of subjectivity that is grounded in the structure elaborated throughout the history of European metaphysics. This structure is the one of appropriation of differences, of totalizing dialectics incorporating the other into the same. As postcolonial critics put it, this linguistic dialectic is a copy—and an active matrix at the same time—of colonial domination, of the process of constituting European identity in relation to the "cultural other," the alien who has to be colonized, civilized, and incorporated into the dominant culture of the empire. The structure of domination and appropriation creates identities of both the colonized and the colonizer, and so does the dialectic inherent in political and philosophical discourses of Europe.[19]

All these domains of power (gaze, knowledge, language, the body) are elements of the process of identity formation in contemporary societies. This kind of approach—a "positive," constructive, as opposed to restrictive, approach to power—has to radically change our understanding of freedom. As Zygmunt Bauman did in relation to gaze, to visual surveillance, the relation of freedom should be analyzed in a broader and more dynamic way than the traditional, negative, liberal approach suggests. If power is more than merely repression, freedom must be something else than lack of repression as well. It seems to me that the dynamics of the process of identity construction are the key factor in the understanding of freedom.

SUBJECTIVITY: BEYOND SUBJECTION

Michel Foucault's thesis that subjectivity is constructed in the process of subjection[20] gains more weight, and slightly changes its meaning in his recent works directly concentrated on the issue of subjectivity. In the last period of his work, Foucault considered subjectivity to be the third major issue, along with knowledge and power, in his attempts to grasp the nature of the contemporary.[21] Acknowledging that the notion of subjectivity has a role to play in theoretical reconstructions of our cultural experience, Foucault weakens the antimodernist edge of his writings. According to Mladen Dolar, in his last lectures Foucault considered the period of the Enlightenment to be more than just a new way of exercising power and oppression: it was also the first epoch to pose the question of its own identity and articulate the task of constructing subjectivity, which ceased to be rooted in divine rules but instead became something to be established within the horizon of the contemporary. Kant's thesis on the separateness of the rational and the political opens up, as Foucault tended to see in his last lectures, a space for a specific kind of freedom grounded in the distance reason can gain from politics, from direct relations of power. Thus divided (the power one must obey, and the reason one can use to question it), the subject is free as long as he or she accepts this dividedness, this internal discontinuity. The idea of the discontinuity of the subject, argues Dolar after Foucault, claimed by postmodern thinkers, is apparently inherent in the very heart of modernity, in Kant's thoughts on the nature of the Enlightenment.[22]

In Foucault's last writings the process of subjectivity construction is analyzed in terms of specific "technologies of the self" grounded in relations of power and knowledge. Contemporary technologies evolved from the ancient ethics of caring for the self, later transformed by the Christian notion of sin implying distance and nonacceptance of the self, and by the technique of confession as a particular procedure of subjectivity construction. In this way language, narration, and verbalization entered the domain of subjectivity formation as constitutive forces. The technology of verbalization is nowadays the dominant technology of the self; a very important arena of its operation is the discourse of the humanities. In human sciences, human nature is actively constructed through verbalization.[23]

Decentration of contemporary power relations makes it necessary for the subject to make use of certain stabilizing factors giving

some coherence to dispersed "subject positions" adopted in relation to particular aspects of power. As Foucault argues in his recent
works, this is an active process on the part of the subject. Subjectivity, therefore, is self-constructed as well as constructed by
external power relations. Let us recall Laclau's notion of representation constructing the sphere of the social, which was presented
in the first chapter of this book. This process seems to be analogical
to verbalization used by individuals in order to construct their
subjectivities. In a very similar way Lawrence Grossberg writes
about the role of ideology in the process of selecting dominant
dimensions of multiple affective investments.[24] In all these ideas
we can see a common assumption that it is the use of language
(verbalization, ideology) that eventually constitutes identity.

Treating the issue of subjectivity as equally important to those
of knowledge and power points to the tendency to overcome the
somehow deterministic heritage of structuralism, still visible in
postmodern theorizing. Recent works by Foucault, the refined
dialectics of postcolonialism, and attentive readings of Derrida
show that the death of the subject was proclaimed too hastily. As
Derrida once put it, he had never said that the subject was to be
dispensed with,

> only that it should be deconstructed. To deconstruct the
> subject does not mean to deny its existence. There are sub-
> jects, "operations" or "effects" of subjectivity. . . . To ac-
> knowledge this does not mean, however, that the subject is
> what it says it is. The subject is not some meta-linguistic
> substance or identity, some pure cogito or self-presence; it is
> always inscribed in language. . . . [Deconstruction] does not,
> therefore, destroy the subject: it simply tries to resituate it.[25]

As Gayatri Spivak notes, logocentrism, in Derrida's work, is
subject to deconstruction, and at the same time it is logocentrism
that enables deconstruction. Logocentric notions—for instance,
the notion of subjectivity—should therefore be a question of
negotiation rather than negation.[26]

The impact of power on the process of subjectivity construction, of decentered, dissolved power inherent in knowledge, gaze, language, and the politics of the body, does not realize itself, therefore, in one-directional transmission, in deterministic impositions. I should say that subjectivity is not so much constructed in power relations as it is in relation to power. The praxis of this process is a fascinating problem, not yet, as it seems, dealt with in a satisfactory way within the discourse of postmodernity. It may have been overlooked as a result of the shocking influence the thesis of the death of the subject has had on the discourse of the humanities; on the other hand, this oversight seems to reflect enormous problems with the articulation of the category of subjectivity in a relational perspective, taking into account both the influence of power relations on the construction of identity and the active positioning of individuals and societies against these relations. If subjectivities were externally, and only externally, constructed, how could they resist power relations? The notion of subjectivity being constructed in power relations challenges the notion of agency that seems inextricable from the notion of resistance. If subjectivities are constructed, there is little basis for burdening individuals with responsibility for their actions; the major condition of responsibility, as is argued within the phenomenological tradition, for instance, is a partial autonomy of the subject.[27] If there is skepticism concerning that autonomy, one of the foundations of ethics is being challenged. In this context it is obvious that the issues of agency and ethics, and therefore of the role of power relations in the process of subjectivity construction, have become the major concern of postmodern emancipatory pedagogy.[28]

I would like to reconsider the process of subjectivity formation in a slightly modified set of relations. As I have mentioned before, I want to emphasize the notion of subjectivity being constructed in relation to power rather than simply in power relations. The basic dynamics of the process, as I assume, consist not in the opposition between being dominated, a passive subjugation, on the one hand, and active resistance, on the other, but, as I now see it, in the dialectic of three basically active processes of positioning oneself against the power. In this sense power relations are both co-created and challenged by the subject. Subjection to power does not mean in such a perspective that an individual does not act, that she or he is reduced to an object of deterministic domination and sometimes surprisingly finds some mysterious basis for agency. Agency "is there" in a way, is part of the process of relatedness, is presupposed in the very notion of relation. I want to stress, however, that the perspective in which subjectivity is considered to be constructed in relation to power rather than simply in power relations—which I am going to develop in this chapter—does not claim to "solve" the problem of subjectivity: the problem remains as mysterious as it has always been. What I am trying to do is to defer the problem, to create a space that would be tentatively free from the metaphysics of subjectivity and thus open to quite simple analyses of the dynamics of relations to power in constructing what we can understand as human identities. In other words, I want to argue that the process of the social construction of identity does not destroy the subject, and that, therefore, it could be renamed as a process of socially based (discursively based, politically based) self-construction. How can this work?

After the deconstruction of Reason, along with widespread attempts to enclose subjectivity within textuality, within discursive practices, there seems to be a theoretical tendency to ground the subject in the body.[29] The body, however culturally constructed itself, has some clear, nondiscursive dimension prior to any textuality. If it can be considered as one of the discourses of subjectivity construction (our bodies are structured in our social experiences; we communicate with our bodies; they signify our social positions; and so on), it is a very particular discourse, a particular site of discursive practices—in a way, a central discourse, the one from which other discourses are read, understood, interpreted, and interrogated. The dialectic tension between the body/subject and other discourses seems to present the first, prior residuum of agency. This is the basis of my attempt to describe subjectivity as constructed in relation to power rather than simply and passively in power relations. There seems always to be a place from which power discourses are actively read, interpreted, and translated into actions.

Let us assume that the process of constructing subjectivity consists in the dynamics of three basic positions, three attitudes to external power, and in the dynamics of relations between these positions. The positions are

1. emulation—action oriented toward the adoption of externally defined signifiers in order to construct one's identity as "not worse" than a "model identity" perceived as bearing the signs of power;

2. mimicry—action oriented toward adopting externally defined signifiers in order to construct one's identity so that it is made invisible, hidden within the dominant code (I am using this concept after Homi Bhabha); and

3. resistance—action oriented toward the inversion of externally defined codes in order to construct one's identity as different from the one defined by the signifiers being imposed by the dominant culture.

Emulation and mimicry replace here what otherwise would be called subjugation; they cover the same scope of behavior, but are considered as active positioning rather than mere results of passive subordination. They are both based upon active recognition of the codes of domination; they are not acts of "surrender." They are part of the process of active self-construction making use of recognized ways of signification linked to those dimensions of dominant culture that are thought to represent aspects of power, of the "superior" identity.

A closer description of this structure requires a gradual presentation of its elements. As it is inspired by ideas derived from postcolonial writings, I will have to introduce some of these concepts first.

In his *White Mythologies: Writing History and the West*, Robert Young undertakes a fascinating attempt to deconstruct the structure of European metaphysics, assuming, after leading representatives of the postcolonial discourse, that the structure of this thought both expresses and projects the structure of colonial rule. Colonial power creates cultural identities of both the colonizer and the colonized. However, as deconstruction of this process interrogates fundamental assumptions of European metaphysics, it is of far greater significance, in my opinion, than classic analyses of colonial power. We can say that colonialism, as described in postcolonial theory, extends relations of power characteristic of nineteenth-century domination over non-European countries. Postcolonialism presents a fundamental critique of Western thought; it is a side look at its tenets, a look from the perspective of what is literally the Third World, from the outside. From that point of view, Western ideologies of domination and those intended to liberate (like Marxism) sometimes look equally oppressive, as long as they share the same basic linguistic and mental structures forming the ontology reflecting the cultural experience of the civilization whose attitude to the world was informed by the practice of conquest and colonization.

The main element of this structure, fully expressed in Hegelian dialectic, and at the same time the main element of the process of identity formation, is the creation of the Other and its subsequent appropriation, its incorporation into the structure of comprehension. The Other is defined by the subject and ascribed to the presumed position of otherness in the dialectic of self-understanding and understanding the world. The classic analysis of this process was presented by Edward Said in his interpretation of the way the West constructed the category of "Orient." The Orient, and orientalism as a discipline of knowledge dealing with it, are based on the ascription of features of otherness (that is, all those features the West does not want to identify "himself" with) to cultures that are basically unknown to Western people. As I already mentioned in chapter 1, the process of cognition in orientalism is rather a kind of recognition, an appropriation of unknown cultures into prepared spaces, previously emptied by exclusions and ready to be filled, in dualistic cognitive structures. Let us recall Derrida's idea of dualistic conceptual structures where the first position is occupied by those concepts that are charged with positive values. In the process of identity formation, the "self" is identified with notions accepted as appropriate, leaving a "shadow," a space of "not-me," the empty space for the Other. What Said stands for is knowledge that considers the objects in their particularity and does not merge them into broad generalizations that carry with them the "violence of ontology," as Young says after Emmanuel Levinas, ontology being a "polished," generalized version of white men's mythology, deprived of sensuality and particularity.[30]

Discussing Said's theory, Young makes a powerful remark concerning the process of identity formation. The creation of the Other is not arbitrary: it is a projection of one's own suppressed, excluded side, one's unaccepted features. Such ascription of one's "dark side," of the unconscious, to a particular culture, group, or individual makes the unconscious real; it creates a social and political reality that is projected out of the unconscious, is objectified, and then—when recognized—challenges one's assumptions concerning the self. According to Young, it was just the structure of the fictional Orient, filled with mystical, emotional, and irrational aspects of European culture, that contributed to the questioning of the rational self-image of Europe. In short, we create the Other according to our unconscious exclusions; then, trying to appropriate it, to include it in our cognitive structures, we are forced to change the notion of our selves.

This process is made still more complicated when the Other starts to behave according to this imposed identity. To describe this aspect of identification, we have to introduce some more notions of postcolonial theory.

The process of identity formation, consisting in the case of dominant cultures in the creation of the Other, in excluding the "not-me," relies in the case of subordinate, "subaltern" cultures on a very complex process of relations with the dominant cultures. These cultures can never be fully appropriated; they do not fit into imposed patterns of otherness and cannot be grasped within the dominant, dualistic logic. The subalterns, as Gayatri Spivak points out, live, in a way, outside the culture; they cannot be narratized, described, or explained. They function like a Derridean "undecidable," something that "is not" in terms of belonging to recognized structures, and that, at the same time, can be identified just because of that structural referent and makes the existence of that referent possible by providing for a "background," for a sphere of otherness. Subaltern groups appear inevitably in the course of any cultural domination. In a way they are a paradoxical condition of the creation of dominant structures. This is clearly visible in the process of theorizing (which is also a way of cultural domination, of imposition of a language that claims to fulfill the demand of comprehension). As Young notes, to construct the class structure of Marxist discourse, one had to exclude those groups whose behavior could not be explained in terms of class relations; therefore "lumpenproletariat" had no place in theoretically sterile Marxist society. Spivak argues that this kind of Derridean "undecidability" is the crucial condition of the strength of subaltern cultures. It is a paradox as well, because these groups are established by the very process of domination; their identities are grounded in exclusions made in the name of dualistic clarity. Attempts to liberate the subaltern, often undertaken by the dominant culture's intellectuals and always implying some form of "enlightenment," of explaining the position of the subaltern within the codes of domination, lead—again paradoxically—to a weakening of their subject positions, or rather to an imposition of a subjectivity that fits in the structural code, that can be conceived and appropriated within a "dominant theory of liberation" that reverses value judgments within the same conceptual frame. Self-consciousness acquired in the practice of such "liberation" leads to the incorporation of the subaltern into the structure of domination.[31] The subaltern, in such a situation, "cannot speak"; there is no subject position he or she could adopt as a place of enunciation.[32] The process of identity formation demands that subalterns reject the logic of domination (as it is this logic that singled them out as a particular group), but negotiate it, adopt a "third," border position that enables them to undertake a cultural translation[33] making it possible to create one's identity within the process of representation,[34] within languages, codes, and ideologies, none of which is their "own."

The notion of translation is one of the crucial concepts in Homi Bhabha's writings.[35] The major concern of Bhabha's theory is the dialectics of mutual relations of dominant and dominated cultures in the process of identity formation. Strongly arguing against the notion of cultural diversity, which places "other" cultures within a space of "common culture" defined by the dominant power, Bhabha says that this kind of cultural politics erases differences between the cultures—differences that are visible on their borders, in complex relations between them. Communication and understanding do not require such unifying notions; cultures do not have to be grounded in a fictional space of sameness. Translation between cultures is possible not because they are similar, but because cultures are signifying, "symbol-forming and subject-constituting interpellative practices."[36] The language of critique, common in every culture (as it is not possible to form cultural identity without critical translation), opens up a "third space," creates a "hybrid" sphere where new features may appear. The process of translation is never one-directional; it is never directed just toward the "alien" culture. Translation affects the self as well; it requires distance from the self and implies a mutual displacement of meanings, and because of the inevitable continuity of translation as the practice of interpellating one's own subjectivity vis-à-vis cultural codes, it results in a constant questionability and hybridity of the subject. As Mikhail Bakhtin put it, "There is no inner, sovereign territory within the human being. He/she is always and all on the border; looking inside, [he] looks into the eyes of the other or through the eyes of the other."[37] As Bhabha claims, such hybridity, such nonsovereignty of the subject, is a condition of political freedom, of an organization of public life that does not presuppose any form of assimilation of dominated cultures. "It is only by losing the sovereignty of the self that one can gain a freedom of politics that is open to the non-assimilationist claims of cultural difference."[38] It is only in such a hybrid, border culture,

Bhabha says, that forms of solidarity may appear, and dualistic opposition between the colonizer and the colonized, between the ruler and the subject, may disappear.

The hybridization of identity is most clearly visible in the analyses of classic colonial relations. The colonized "other," being a creation of the dominant culture, forms his or her identity in a process of mimicry, around signifiers related to the dominant power, as if trying to make himself or herself invisible, not different from the colonizer. This process never leads, however, to a total similarity. What emerges instead is a hybrid, a parody, a displaced caricature of the colonial identity. The gaze of the colonizer creates the colonized, but instead of encountering the alien Other, its own creation reflecting the dialectic of exclusions, it meets the colonizer's own distorted reflection, his caricature. Gaze loses its power; in constructing the Other, the colonizer deprives himself of the basis of exercising control and creates conditions that eventually may lead to a peculiar balance, to a suspension of domination, to a total immersion in overwhelming hybridity. Mimicry, which appears to follow the expectations of the colonizer, can therefore paradoxically result in disempowering the dominant power and create conditions for active resistance. What comes next is a paranoia of the colonizer, a constant distrust and insecurity ("they hate us," "they lie") that often leads to overt aggression, but also to the hybridization of the identity of the colonizer, to displacements blurring his notion of the self.[39]

Such analyses shed new light on the process of identity formation in relations of power and in relation to power. Let us note that mimicry is an active process, not merely a subordination. It is self-construction based upon both alienation from one's own culture and translation of the dominant one. The hybrid that emerges out of this process is not only a new individuality of the colonized, but also a challenge to the identity of the dominant culture, a challenge to the colonizer, a displacement of the meaning of his subjectivity.

The dynamics of power and identity, as described by Bhabha, can be treated in a broader way. In scattered analyses of the process of identity construction one can sometimes find descriptions of similar actions, but motivated by a different desire, the one of emulation, of proving one's value in terms of dominant cultural codes. Such actions are assertive by nature and thus often aggressive in motive, driven by hatred of the dominant power. Still, their outcomes may appear very close to the demands of that power, albeit equally as hybrid and ambiguous as those described by Bhabha.

Emulation is a striving to be "not worse" than someone whose superiority is tacitly implied in its very nature. Abigail Solomon-Godeau provides an interesting case of such a situation in her analysis of Connie Hatch's series of photographs accompanied by recorded stories told by their heroines. Hatch's exhibition was called "Serving the Status Quo." A part of the series is about Frankie, a lesbian feminist who totally rejects all aspects of male domination and is very sensitive to any visible sign of it. Rejecting the female role imposed by the male-dominated culture, Frankie unconsciously identifies herself with numerous attributes of masculinity: she is an independent professional, wears very short hair and "male" shirts and trousers, drinks beer, and displays all kinds of "male" behavior. Her image, as presented in the photographs, is very "masculine." In one of her comments Frankie says that if she had anything of a male in her, she would commit suicide.

The process of identity formation documented by Hatch and analyzed by Solomon-Godeau is very interesting. The rejection of male domination results in a need of emulation, of proving one's own "not-worseness" to oneself. That in turn demands the acceptance of visual clues characteristic of the dominant culture as the basis of one's own identity. All this leads to what Solomon-Godeau calls "sexual identity as a form of masquerade." Frankie and other heroines of Hatch's photographs become "totally absorbed in the task of adapting themselves to match the model of desire."[40] As in Bhabha's theory, we can see here a hybrid, an "impossible identity" full of unresolvable conflicts and contradictions. Solomon-Godeau notices one more interesting thing: Frankie's story produces equally conflicted, "hybrid" reactions from the public of the exhibition. As in Bhabha, again, hybridity and masquerade result in displacements in the identities of the people who identify themselves with such parodied roles. There is a difference, however. If Bhabha's mimicry is a kind of refuge where the colonized hides from the gaze within the codes of the dominant culture, which makes her or him invisible and in a way "unmanageable," Frankie's identity is clearly oriented toward spectacular transgression, toward a rupturing as visible as can be of the code fixing her social status.

Resistance in a way presents the other side of the mechanisms of emulation and mimicry—in a way, because it is rather difficult to draw a clear border between them. Mimicry, as analyzed by Bhabha, makes the colonial gaze impotent and opens up possibilities of resistance; adaptation, as described by Solomon-Godeau and here referred to as emulation, is legitimized by oppositional, subversive hatred. Both these ways of coping with power look as if they were just one-dimensional subjugation, a total failure to retain one's "own," "authentic" identity in relations with dominant culture. On the other hand, oppositional behaviors displayed as violent actions, looking like acts of resistance, may result in eventual subordination to the dominant power. The ethnography by Paul Willis that analyzes the outcomes of student rebellion is a classic example here.[41] In contemporary critical pedagogy the notion of resistance is far more complicated and refined. It takes into account the need of not just "acting back," inverting dominant codes, but of overcoming them through a critical distance requiring particular competencies and in critical action developing an ethical project.[42] However, in one-dimensional relations, if we can imagine them while forgetting for a moment about the "universality of the border" (to borrow the term from Lech Witkowski), resistance seems to consist of searching for ways of self-exclusion from the relations of domination, mostly through exhibiting behavior prohibited by the power. In this way a space of relative freedom can be gained, although it will be the freedom of inversion, in a way prescribed by the resisted power, confined to its codes, and defined in advance for those who "feel like resisting it."

Concluding this part of my presentation, and preparing ground for the next part, I would like to propose the following thesis: the process of positioning oneself against the power, taking place on the level of relations defined by the power, leads to an incorporation of the individual into the structures of domination and at the same time into some form and some scope of freedom, where subjects can make choices and construct their identities by making use of signs provided by the dominant discourse (note Bauman's notion of consumerist freedom linked to the political, economic, and cultural domination of the corporate capitalist state). This thesis seems to be relevant to identifications constructed on the basis of mimicry and emulation as well as of resistance, as long as they do not exceed the level of discourse defined by the dominant culture. However, as a result of such identifications, there always seems to emerge a "third," hybrid, border identity overcoming the prescribed matrix of subjectivity formation. This outcome opens up possibilities of different forms of freedom, not defined and not foreseen within the discourse of power, forms of subjectivity and of subjugation. Hybridity of the identity constructed in relation to power opens up the space of change.

Education, and particularly emancipatory education, is addressed to that sphere of incomplete, hybrid identities. This is the sphere of openness, of a "not-yet," of critique and of translation; and it is at the same time the sphere of desire of oneness, unity, and ideological closure, the sphere of desire of certainty and order. This is the sphere where education does make a difference.

In the following part I want to illustrate this structure of identity formation (that is power and relation to power, emulation/mimicry/resistance, hybridity, and emancipation), dealing with it in terms of dimensions of power. Let us try to see this process in the panorama of contemporary agents of power: from the perspectives of the Eye, the Body, the Tongue, and Knowledge.

THE EYE OF THE POWER

If power is based on gaze, looks are the base of identity. We can find some support for this idea in Bauman's *Freedom* and in some investigations into popular culture. Douglas Kellner writes: "In a postmodern image culture, individuals get their very identity from these [advertised] figures; thus advertising becomes an important and overlooked mechanism of socialization as well as [a] manager of consumer demands."[43]

Visual surveillance, supported by role, status, and prestige clues encoded in popular culture, sets in motion a process of constructing personal images in such a way that they communicate certain messages concerning identifications, aspirations, and affective investments to the social environment. By buying and wearing clothes, having our hair styled, and carrying shopping bags, we communicate with others, we display our identities, and we legitimize ourselves as pertinent persons in given places. This would be the first, "uncritical" level of visual identity constructed on the basis of ready-to-use items acquired in commercial institutions relevant to our social statuses. The mechanism of such identifications is widely used in advertising, sometimes in a way that reveals a total lack of a nonsymbolic significance of goods suggested as objects of purchase. In some supermarkets discount goods (attractive in terms of price, but not attractive as signs of status) are labelled "just as advertised on TV." Let us note the relation between the signified and signifiers in this slogan: a concrete, physical object, supposedly of some use value, is presented as a sign—and only a sign—of a "reality" of television commercials. The paradox here is only apparent. Buying goods in consumer societies is first of all a symbolic action, an act of constructing, affirming, and communicating one's identity. Therefore it is relevant to refer these acts to the sphere of cultural codes associating images with values, rather than to practical needs. It is as well a free act, an act of choice—within strictly set limits, however. Trespassing seems to be "prosecuted" in a form of blurred personal image making social identity unclear and social relations more complicated.

Still, trespassing is a common phenomenon. Let us take another look at this kind of ad. It clearly seems to appeal to contradictory drives: on the one hand, to getting things cheap, and on the other, to getting a sign of high status (something advertised on TV is potentially an object of desire of the many). As this way of selling discount goods is quite common, it points to what must be assumed to be a widespread desire of emulation, of self-presentation driven by the motive of being "not worse." As we can see, this act of individual transgression is socially and institutionally foreseen and, at least to some extent, constructed within the system of mass communication. Thus a created hybrid identity can be immediately subjected to further colonization and, through the same appeal to the will of emulation, set back into a prepared, visibly marked status of a person who "wants to appear different," as she or he apparently does not like who she or he is.

What are the possibilities of avoiding the gaze? The simplest one seems to be an escape into privacy. Closing the door and blinding the windows makes it possible to "undress," to remove visual clues worn for the sake of the gaze. The intimacy of the home seems to point to the intensity of the gaze. However, intimacy is also becoming a sphere of control, especially for those who are excluded from the space of consumerist freedom of choice, for the poor. This was also the case in Communist states, where welfare institutions, to say nothing of police, had more access to people's homes than was common in democratic consumer societies. I say "was" because new technologies of data processing have made direct access to private lives trivially easy.

Hiding from the gaze can also take the form of hiding among the others or behind signs of otherness. These seem to be more active forms of resisting the gaze, demanding some expertise in deciphering dominant codes of identification and codes of resistance. Mimicry can be oriented toward either of these codes. We can adopt signs of dominant "sameness," thus hiding within what seems to be invisible, or, on the contrary, we can use visible, bright, aggressive signs of "otherness," of counterculture, of rebellion. In the first case the process of hybridization follows Bhabha's description; in the second one it makes use of the inevitable commercialization of countercultural phenomena, of their inscription into the logic of the market. The rebellion is over and becomes safely accessible when everybody can buy a badge, a T-shirt, or a poster in order to display his or her rebel identity. The subaltern, the Other with no name, becomes a labelled object of surveillance the very day when he or she decides to make his or her identity visible.

Resistance against the gaze takes most visibly the form of inverting it. The domain of popular culture returns the gaze of the power; it provides for at least fictional means of fixing the looks, the visual identity of those in higher ranks of power. Their images are constructed in soap operas, in gossip columns, in gutter press scandals, and in TV news and talk shows hungry for intimate details that disclose the sphere of privacy and make the homes of the mighty transparent and insecure. Postmodern surveillance affects all, and only sometimes does our need of clarity make us believe that there must be some hidden power behind the visible structures of the economic and political establishment, not subject to the public gaze. The search for these "secret agents of power" in popular media (foreign intelligence, the Mafia, and so on) proves once again that the power of gaze, like all powers, is decentered, that it is exercised by everybody.

THE BODY OF THE SUBJECT

As long as contemporary power has the eye, it apparently, as Michel Foucault suggests, has no body. Power is in structures, invisible; instead it makes clear demands concerning the bodies of its subjects. I have already mentioned Foucault's notion of biopower concerning all corporal features important in terms of the reason of state. In this perspective the body is important as long as it is an element of the population, of the state's biological resources.[44] Demands concerning the body are stated clearly in health politics (note that health is a political matter), in welfare institutions, and, last but not least, in education.[45] The politics of the body is also a crucial element of popular culture and its politics of representation.[46] These external forces of body production (education, health politics, cultural representations) are met by internal drives to construct one's body—one's discursive, signifying body—from within, from its prelinguistic layers of sensibility. In this process signifiers provided by the discourses of power are used to supplement the basic structure of desire with structures of meaning. How, in this perspective, can we outline the process of identity formation, of constructing the "body/subject" in terms of the dynamics of mimicry, emulation, and resistance?

First we should note a direct relation between this question and the question of visual identity. Some aspects of this problem, however, seem to exceed the issue of visuality. Second, we should remember a general feature of the contemporary political control: its apparent invisibility. One of the central aspects of the politics of the body, therefore, will be the concealment of its sense, its self-presentation rendering inherent mechanisms of control invisible.

In brief I think that it is possible to summarize contemporary writings on the politics of the body and state that its major concern is to construct identities based upon the following features: youth, physical aptitude, sexual attractiveness, and invisibility of differences (that is, sexual, racial, and other differences are presented as basically irrelevant). In popular culture apparently dominant messages appeal to strength and power (masculinity rather than feminity, visible marks of high social status, able-bodiedness). They create the image of a person who controls everything that concerns his (and it is mainly his) life. The intersection of youthfulness and power creates a particular attitude to death: in the politics of representation death appears in the form of killing (active, powerful, a way of exercising control over the other) rather than dying (passive, painful, vulnerable in terms of dependency on the other, an outright negation of the mass-media-promised land of eternal youth and joy). Dying and suffering, the perspective of the end, of existential fear that makes us dependent on the presence of other people and makes us open to questions of meaning, form a visible sphere of exclusions both in American popular culture (TV series or everyday conversations ruled by the obligation to "feel fine") and in the practice of health and welfare institutions (death behind a curtain, in hospitals, out of sight). As I have mentioned earlier, Michel Foucault clearly points to the relation between biopolitics—the politics of health—and the trope of dying, the politics of death. Institutionalized and nationalized health politics appeared on the European scene precisely at the time when total wars engaging whole nations also appeared. It is a reason of state that makes demands on the part of the "population" to die for the country, and on the part of the administration to take care of the health of it.[47] In the politics of representation, and in the practice of identity formation, the "health" part of this political structure is emphasized, while the "death" part is erased.

Let us try to point to the elements of mimicry, emulation, and resistance in the practice of identity formation in relation to biopower. It seems that mimicry, self-formation through the acquisition of signifiers offered by the dominant culture, and emulation, a similar process with the motive of being "not worse" than the idols of power, are based mainly on the notion of power and control over one's own body. The care for the body is institutionalized and commercialized to the extent of enabling individuals to intellectually control physical endeavors in terms of energy expenditure and to measure weight, muscular strength, and the amount of particular nutrients consumed in grocery goods. This way of caring is accompanied by the demise, strikingly visible in American culture, of "natural" forms of physical activity like walking, using stairs, and so on, unless it is walking "for health," that is, in a specially designed time, space, and sporting equipment, or using stairs in a gym where a counter can keep track of every step one makes. This is a relatively benign form of cultural hybridity of the body, and one can point to more controversial ones, like attempts to fully, rationally control one's biological functions. In the politics of representation those who are perceived as epitomes of wealth, health, and success seem to live outside time. Even if they grow old, they are still sexually attractive; they hardly ever fall ill or grow fat. To emulate these cultural patterns means to fight against one's own body. Such emulation may result in denying one's age, sexuality, race, and even death in the hope that someone in the future will want to cure the defrosted flesh. The notion of total control over the body is also visible in the heated discussion on the issues of abortion and test-tube fertilization. Serious as these issues are, they do represent a form of biohybridity, of a "third," negotiable, unclear, and uncertain sphere that is neither purely biological nor merely cultural, and at the same time is doubtless political.

Mechanisms of resistance, of negative body/subject formation in relation to biopower, seem to comprise two main motives: the lack of control over the body (as in obscene trespassing of various "physiological taboos," lack of control over emotions and desires—aggression, overt sexuality, gluttony, and the whole array of other "sins") and self-destruction. In this sense the use of drugs and alcohol, smoking, or risking one's life in dangerous entertainments or fights may be understood as a sign of striving for negative freedom, for independence from the invisible biopower. As in previously discussed ways of resistance, such gestures seem to be foreseen by the dominant force and hardly challenge its power of control. Eventually such bioresisters end up in hospitals, prisons, unemployment offices, welfare shelters, and other institutions of political care over their bodies.

THE TONGUE

The power of the language, or the power exercised through the language, can be conceived in two basic dimensions: that of categorization (stating the objects of cognitive activities, giving them names), and—as I have already mentioned—that of valuation of the categories based on the dualistic and asymmetric structure of meaning, placing positively valued concepts in the first position in every pair. In a particular contemporary way this power is wielded, as Foucault suggests in his *Technologies of the Self,* in the form of "verbalization," as a modern technology of subjectivity construction.

The subjective response to the power of language can have the form of mimicry, of taking over the mechanism of control and using it in the process of self-construction. The acquisition of language and of its semantic structures gives an individual a possibility of control over cognitive representations of the world and the self. One may give names instead of being merely named;

one may enunciate in order to reverse the dominant language, that is, use the same language while depriving it of intentionally inscribed meanings; and so on. The clearest example of such a situation would be the colonized using the colonial language, actively employing its categorical function and inevitably displacing the meanings, giving them new and unpredicted shape. Of course, in power relations taking place within one ethnic group this process loses some of its clarity, but still, as I think, it can be observed. It is sufficient to recall linguistic hybrids appearing in intergenerational relations or in the classroom where students try to adopt "pedagogical" language in order to control the conversational exchange with the teacher.

The technique of verbalization employed in the process of subjectivity construction creates a particular sphere: the sphere of unconsciousness. This results from the impossibility of full verbalization of experience. Verbalization leads to closures, "squeezes" experience into discrete verbal units, and creates distance between such separated meanings. There is always something left aside, something not exactly labelled, not properly named, something in between distinguishable signifiers. If consciousness is of linguistic nature, these excluded spheres of experience create the basis for unconsciousness. The unconscious results also from the dualistic structure of categorization. Every category we use to identify our subjectivity, that is, to create our identity, has its "shadow," its negation that corresponds to the sphere of potential exclusions, to the identification of "not-me." In this way we develop a readiness to construct the Other, to build a stereotype of otherness that can be employed in constructing visions of the unknown. Moreover, by adopting the dominant, and therefore to some extent "ideologically frozen," coherent language and employing the technique of verbalization in the process of self-construction, we actively contribute to the creation of social reality. Exclusions inherent in this process are carried into the sphere of social relations by our identities. In this way we become part of the chain of power; we transmit linguistically imposed political exclusions and create "real" others. It seems that it is our linguistically identified subjectivities, our "verbal" (or, more broadly, cultural) identities that carry on decentered power relations in the way Foucault described.[48]

Resistance against the power of language seems to be possible either in the form of creating a new language, or through avoidance of verbalization. A new language can be based, for example, on reversed structures of valuation. Jonathan Rutherford provides an interesting analysis of such cases in his study of the process of identity formation of oppositional movements. Slogans like "Black Is Beautiful," "Gay Pride," and others reverse the dominant word order and place "bad" or "weak" words in the first place, supplementing them with "strong" words placed in "weak" positions.[49] In a way a new language appears in gender-sensitive linguistic practices of feminist writing that rupture the signifying codes through the replacement of predominant male pronouns with female ones, as in compound sentences where "man" becomes "she." Resistance based on attempts to create new linguistic practices seems commonplace in dominated communities and societies, in prisons, classrooms, army units, or colonized nations. Such attempts are something more than mere acts of coding the process of communication so as to hide it from the "ear of the power"; they are also attempts to categorize the world differently, to ascribe values to the categories in another way, and to form identities on the basis of other, oppositional counterdiscourses and countervalues. In this process the mechanism of exclusion is maintained and employed as broadly as possible: the colonizer is constructed as the Other, or the group seeks for others within. It seems well documented that these new categorizations and oppositional valuations are often inversions of the dominant ones, and that the structure of domination and exclusions is usually not addressed in the process of inversion.[50]

The second possibility seems to rely on grounding the process of identity construction in affects, emotions, and desires rather than in verbally identified concepts. Emotions are either deliberately separated from the practice of naming or are named "idiosyncratically," labelled without a possibility of incorporation into larger signifying structures. When emotions are used in the process of identity construction, as in poetry, lovers' communication, or religion, they are labelled with specially invented words or with words whose meaning is strictly limited to those experiences, and thus they retain their features of "authenticity." Experiences without names, or with names that refer to nothing except them, cannot be systematized and therefore cannot be set one against another; the self constructed on their basis may not imply the Other.

In a way this kind of self-construction is an attempt to build one's identity around the notion of authenticity. Is this possible, though? Some current ideas pose serious doubts in this matter. First, let us recall those beliefs that stress the linguistic nature of the psyche, its culturally constructed character. All aspects of subjectivity appear there to be culturally rather than individually constructed. As Stuart Hall points out, identity is constructed within the process of representation. Derrida, Lacan, and Heidegger all stress some form of linguistic determination of subjectivity. In Heidegger the notion of authenticity is eventually reduced to understanding one's own unauthenticity and implies some intellectualization of experience. If avoidance of verbalization is thought to resist the power of language in order to retain some kind of authentic freedom of the self, it is also considered to bear some kind of basically "unauthentic," linguistically shaped structural dualism as well. The structure of the language is thus duplicated in the act of resistance through the very opposition of "authentic" (natural, biologically grounded, pure, not intermediated) affects and desires and "unauthentic" (cultural, grounded in the language, socially intermediated) technologies of verbalization. The opposition to unauthenticity, to a possibility of "being named," either by others or by oneself, clearly points to the conceptual dimension of authenticity thus enacted. Authenticity and unauthenticity themselves make a pair, a conceptual, dualistic opposition. Authenticity is thus based on the structure of negation it claims to avoid. All this process seems to lead to the same paralinguistic structure of binary oppositions and, consequently, to some practice of social exclusions based on the condemnation of "unauthentic life."

KNOWLEDGE

To consider the question of knowledge in a proper way would require summarizing all previously analyzed dimensions of power relations. In the poststructural perspective, knowledge is power; it is also more than traditionally conceived rational, verbalized information. Let us recall popular knowledge, body (or "carnal") knowledge, and so on. Such a broadening of the notion of knowledge has to do, on the one hand, with its relation to the contemporary concept of power, and, on the other, with the change in the way we think about subjectivity, with the abandonment of the notion of a rational, integrated, and autonomous person using his or her conceptual thinking to make independent decisions.

Without distinguishing between various kinds of knowledge (popular versus scientific, rational versus carnal, and so on), I would like to concentrate now on just one feature of the dynamics of its functioning in power relations. Power, which is always a process of knowledge production, a "regime of truth," is at the same time a process of distributing the unknown, of the "un-knowledge," of ignorance production. Let us note what is the role of uncertainty whether one is or is not observed at a given moment (as in Bentham's *Panopticon*), in the process of internalization of mechanisms of surveillance. The distinction between knowledge and ignorance and the fact of uneven distribution of knowledge are, however, hidden in relations of domination, according to the rule of "invisibility of ideology." In other words, what is hidden is at the same time erased; its lack of presence is rendered invisible. One does not know what one does not know. As a result, what individuals know, they are made to consider true: what they know constitutes the world and their identities. Such knowledge cannot be questioned easily from the perspective of silence, ignorance, and structured "un-knowledge."

In the process of identity formation, the structural opposition between knowledge and ignorance can become the basis for an emulative desire for erudition, a desire to "know everything." Someone who manages to realize the limited character of his or her knowledge may develop a need for a "larger" knowledge perceived as a mark of higher social and political status. This desire implies a hierarchical notion of knowledge, comprising broader scopes of information on subsequent levels of power, of the potential to control the reality. The desire of erudition implies that to know more is to have more power. Individuals constructing their identities in relation to this desire will probably gain more and more knowledge made accessible for them and visibly related to the image of power. This is bound to be a "positive" knowledge that concerns "what is" rather than "what is not." It will not embrace what was subject to omission or silencing, what was deprived of the status of legitimate knowledge. "Un-knowledge" is deprived of representation linking it with attributes of power and therefore may not seem attractive for an "emulating" identity. This attractiveness of positive knowledge and invisibility of ignorance make it difficult for those subject to the power of knowledge to develop competencies of critical thinking.

Mimicry seems to be a weaker version of this kind of learning. Accessible knowledge is duly acquired, but without a visible desire to "know all." What we can see instead is rather a tendency not to ask questions, to make do with what is given, to take it for granted. One of the outcomes of this attitude may be a dogmatization of knowledge, a belief that there is no other knowledge to acquire. One may adopt the imposed worldview, construct one's identity according to granted beliefs, and become an "invisible person," an identity without distinctive features. Such a rigid system of beliefs, built upon a limited scope of knowledge, from the point of view of the dominant culture, with dogmatic claims to understand everything (Are these beliefs fake, staged just for the sake of the colonizer? This is the paranoid problem of the dominant power.), creates an uncontrollable hybrid resistant to further endeavors of "informational management" and ideally transmitting the mechanism of power, an ideal bureaucratic clerk of a lower rank.

Resistance against knowledge can be conceived as "active ignorance," as refusal to know. In the Lacanian psychoanalysis ignorance is different from the mere lack of knowledge; it is an active process based on the dynamics of identity and negativity, of linguistic "closures" and negative openness. As Satya Mohanty points out, knowledge can be an obstacle to knowing, a limitation on access to the reality of experience.[51] Structuring, categorizing functions of knowledge exclude from the process of cognition precisely as much as they include. Knowledge about "what it is" is at the same time about "what it is not," and that "is not" is erased as an object of further investigation, of the desire to know. In this context ignorance removes the "obstacle of knowledge," it opens the way to the process of Being and can be understood as a result of the desire of freedom, as a form of negativity that constitutes human nature along with the process of identity formation. Madan Sarup wrote about this Lacanian dialectic:

> Negativity is the negation of identity. Human beings are truly free or really human only in and by effective negation of the given real. Negativity, then, is nothing other than human freedom. The freedom which is realized and manifested as dialectical or negating action is thereby a creation. What is involved is not replacing one given by another given, but overcoming the given in favor of what does not (yet) exist. In short, man is neither identity nor negativity alone but totality or synthesis; that is, he "overcomes" himself while preserving and sublimating himself.[52]

Another mechanism of resistance against knowledge can be conceived as the setting of one form of knowledge against another. For instance, school knowledge can be rejected when it is recognized as contradictory to the "out-of-school" experience. Affective investments located in areas excluded from the legitimate scope of knowledge transmitted in the process of education can be defended at the expense of school knowledge. In extreme cases this kind of resistance in defense of one's own cultural capital may result in a total negation of schooling, in abandoning the dominant culture, and in a kind of closure within one's cultural tradition. This is the case of Paul Willis's "lads" reaffirming their cultural capital at the expense of emancipatory possibilities offered by the process of schooling and thus contributing to the process of cultural reproduction.[53]

At this point I would like to summarize these attempts to understand the process of identity formation in relation to power. I think that we can distinguish between three basic kinds of activities of the subject in relation to power structures in the process of identity formation: emulation (an assertive action that leads to the adoption of signs of the dominant culture in order to achieve at least apparently higher social status defined by the power relations), mimicry (an action that also leads to the adoption of the signs of the dominant culture, but without a clear desire of higher status, oriented rather toward survival and invisibility within the dominant codes), and resistance (action countering the dominant often, if not by nature, involving inversion of meanings and valuations).

All these strategies, in all respective dimensions of power relations, comprise behaviors defined by these relations. They are actions within a determined space. At the same time they can bring about a specific kind of freedom; they create a sphere of control over given aspects of reality, or a sphere of independence from external control—a sphere of positive and negative freedom. Marks of higher social status acquired through emulation may affect how individuals perceive themselves, and how they are perceived by others. That in turn may directly affect the ability to exercise control over one's environment. Visible resistance against certain aspects of subjection, and constructing one's identity around the notion of independence, may also result in some broadening of the sphere of individual choices. A particular kind of negative freedom appears as a result of mimicry. This acquired freedom from gaze, "invisibility," confines an individual to the shelter built within the dominant code; it is a freedom in a hideaway.

It seems that particularly (and perhaps only) the latter kind of freedom, gained as a result of mimicry, creates a situation providing for a transmission of relations of power by a subjectivity that has been constructed within the code of domination. This thesis would make Foucault's notion of power relations more contextual and restricted to a particular kind of subject formation. In the other two cases relations of power are maintained in the process of identity construction; they are not challenged or questioned in a significant way, but they do not seem to be actively reinforced either. A "pure" transmission, as I think, is only possible in a mimic immersion of a person within a code, where she or he becomes impersonal and invisible (and thus to some extent uncontrollable, which may be the main motive behind this kind of identification). When individual enunciation makes a person thus constructed visible, it hides the code; power relations are then hidden behind a "human," personalized performance. Mimicry frees individuals from gaze and thus makes them ideal, "transparent" supervisors. This kind of hybridity was analyzed by Homi Bhabha with reference to ethnic clerks and servants working as middlemen in the process of colonization. I think, however, that this kind of mimic identity can be understood as a crucial link, a transmission belt in all relations of domination.

Identity construction in relation to power provides for a certain scope of freedom, even though this kind of freedom is defined by these relations of power. However, the situations described here seem to lead to some transgression; they create hybrid, unforeseen subjectivities, a kind of "neither-nor" identities constructed between dominant and subjugated discourses. There is some tragic, schizoid tension in such a subjectivity stretched between conflicting systems of values and significations, making the identity nonsovereign, as Homi Bhabha calls it. According to Bhabha, nonsovereign identity can be a crucial element of the struggle for another freedom, a political freedom of solidarity, free from the danger of homogenizing unification that suppresses differences in the name of "common culture" embracing cultural diversity. The hybridity of the subject is, therefore, a condition of transgression, of social change, of cultural openness. This kind of subjectivity (multiple, amorphous, amoebic, hybrid, schizoid)—as many claim, the typical subjectivity of our times, being a result of numerous struggles over meanings and values, of attempts to come to terms in either way with relations of power and domination—is the addressee of education.

The notion of a nonsovereign subject seems to be in contradiction to the idea of freedom in its liberal, individualistic articulation. However, it is this "antihumanist" notion that makes it possible to introduce ethical questions into the discourse of subjectivity. Bhabha says that such subjectivity liberates the politics of solidarity. Young, in his commentary on postcolonial theory, quotes Emmanuel Levinas, who suggested that the "much lamented" ontological subject be replaced in the discourse of the humanities by the notion of the ethical subject open to the Other without a desire of incorporation. Subjectivity is, then, ethically, not ontologically, grounded. You do not have to know who you are in order to say "I am here" when someone cries for help. It is this kind of ethical relatedness that makes us human.[54]

Openness to forms of noninclusive, noncolonial engagement, to solidarity, makes it possible for individuals to position themselves within a community and thus to engage in the process of its location in the external world. In this way people can adopt an extratextual, experiential position temporarily identifying their subjectivities, a "closure" of the flux of subjective hybridity, an ideological standing from which discursive practices can be questioned and criticized. Individuals and communities thus gain "textual power" stemming from the social positioning against discursive practices and can engage in practices of critique, of creating "texts against the text"—which always requires, as Robert Scholes argues, this kind of social, political, extratextual location as the place of articulation.[55] Through the social positioning, social anchorage, and textual power thus developed, individuals and communities can develop a notion of agency that enables them to responsibly choose between textual practices and freely interrogate them, taking control over textuality with its claims to construct their subject positions and identities.

The ethical dimension of subjectivity is a central issue in Henry Giroux's theory of education. This pedagogy aims to formulate a project of education based on nonfundamentalist ethics of solidarity and difference. Other postmodern projects address other issues, but they all in some way, directly or indirectly, presuppose the hybrid, relational subject, not fully defined, and stretched between contradictory significations. Let us note that this subject does already have his or her individual freedom elaborated in numerous struggles within the field defined by power relations. Emancipatory pedagogy, therefore, is not merely about making people free; it does not offer freedom instead of enslavement. What is at stake here is far more complex and difficult: it is the task of making freedom problematic, of interrogating personal freedom of the self coping with the power, self-constructed in relation to power, and of making the inevitable hybridity of the subject open and accepted in its openness. It is in this openness that the ethical grounding for social freedom lies. The political project of emancipatory pedagogy is in this perspective particularly radical.

In the next chapter I will briefly consider some curriculum projects of postmodern pedagogy. I will consider what kind of freedom is presupposed in them, and how it is related to the ontological freedom conceded to individuals in their relations to power, in their struggles over meanings defined within these relations and in relation to them.

NOTES

1. Isaiah Berlin, quoted in Peter Gay, "Freud and Freedom: On a Fox in Hedgehog's Clothing," in Alan Ryan, ed., *The Idea of Freedom* (Oxford: Oxford University Press, 1979), p. 55.

2. Maxine Greene, *The Dialectic of Freedom* (New York: Teachers College Press, 1988), p. 3.

3. See, for example, Henry A. Giroux, *Schooling and the Struggle for Public Life: Critical Pedagogy in the Modern Age* (Minneapolis: University of Minnesota Press, 1988).

4. Roger Simon, "For a Pedagogy of Possibility," *Critical Pedagogy Networker* 1, no. 1 (1988): 2.

5. See, for example, Carl Rogers, *Freedom to Learn for the 80's* (Columbus, Ohio: Charles E. Merrill, 1983).

6. See Henry A. Giroux, "Theories of Reproduction and Resistance in the New Sociology of Education," *Harvard Educational Review* 53, no. 3 (1983): 257–293; *Theory and Resistance in Education* (South Hadley, Mass.: Bergin and Garvey, 1983).

7. Michel Foucault, *Power/Knowledge: Selected Interviews and Other Writings, 1972–1977* (New York: Pantheon Books, 1980), p. 97.

8. Michel Foucault, quoted in Robert Young, *White Mythologies: Writing History and the West* (London: Routledge, 1990), p. 9.

9. Zygmunt Bauman, *Freedom* (Minneapolis: University of Minnesota Press, 1988).

10. Ibid., p. 63.

11. Ibid., p. 85.

12. Ibid., p. 93.

13. Ibid. However, the notion of autonomy needs careful reconsideration. It is burdened with meanings that make the postmodern project of emancipation problematic. I will refer to this issue in the last chapter.

14. I am using the term "body/subject" after Peter McLaren. See, for example, "Schooling the Postmodern Body: Critical Pedagogy and the Politics of Enfleshment," in Henry A. Giroux, ed., *Postmodernism, Feminism, and Cultural Politics: Redrawing Educational Boundaries* (Albany: State University of New York Press, 1991), pp. 144–173; "On Ideology and Education: Critical Pedagogy and the Cultural Politics of Resistance," in Henry A. Giroux and Peter McLaren, eds., *Critical Pedagogy, the State, and Cultural Struggle* (Albany: State University of New York Press, 1989), pp. 174–202.

15. See, for example, Lawrence Grossberg, "Teaching the Popular," in Cary Nelson, ed., *Theory in the Classroom* (Urbana: University of Illinois Press, 1986).

16. Robert Scholes, *Textual Power: Literary Theory and the Teaching of English* (New Haven, Conn.: Yale University Press, 1985).

17. "If psychoanalysis is to be constituted as the science of the unconscious, one must set out from the notion that the unconscious is structured like a language. From this I have deduced a topology intended to account for the constitution of the subject." Jacques Lacan, *The Four Fundamental Concepts of Psycho-analysis* (New York: W. W. Norton, 1981), p. 203. For an account of Lacan's theory, see, for example, Madan Sarup, *An Introductory Guide to Post-structuralism and Postmodernism* (Athens: University of Georgia Press, 1989).

18. Stuart Hall, "Cultural Identity and Diaspora," in Jonathan Rutherford, ed., *Identity: Community, Culture, Difference* (London: Lawrence and Wishart, 1990), p. 222.

19. See Young, *White Mythologies*, pp. 12–14.

20. Foucault, *Power/Knowledge*, p. 97.

21. See L. H. Martin, H. Gutman, and P. H. Hutton, eds., *Technologies of the Self: A Seminar with Michel Foucault* (Amherst: University of Massachusetts Press, 1988), pp. 9–15.

22. Mladen Dolar, "The Legacy of the Enlightenment: Foucault and Lacan," *New Formations*, no. 14 (1991): pp. 43–56.

23. Michel Foucault, "The Political Technology of Individuals," in L. H. Martin, H. Gutman, and P. H. Hutton, eds., *Technologies of the Self: A Seminar with Michel Foucault* (Amherst: University of Massachusetts Press, 1988), pp. 175–162.

24. Grossberg, "Teaching the Popular."

25. Jacques Derrida, "Deconstruction and the Other," in Richard Kearney, *Dialogues with Contemporary Continental Thinkers: The Phenomenological Heritage* (Manchester, England: Manchester University Press, 1984), p. 125.

26. Gayatri Ch. Spivak, *The Post-Colonial Critic: Interviews, Strategies, Dialogues*, ed. Sarah Harasym (New York: Routledge, 1990), p. 147.

27. See, for example, Roman Ingarden, *Man and Value* (München: Philosophia Verlag, 1983).

28. See for example, Giroux, *Schooling and the Struggle for Public Life*.

29. The discourse of the body is taken up by Peter McLaren in his numerous writings on subjectivity and education. See, for example, Peter McLaren, *Schooling as a Ritual Performance: Towards a Political Economy of Educational Symbols and Gestures* (London: Routledge and Kegan Paul, 1986).

30. This trace in Young's text leads to Derrida's analyses of metaphysics. In one of his texts Derrida uses Anatole France's metaphor describing philosophers polishing coins in order to "discover" pure gold beneath the surface drawings; such "deep truth" erases all traces of sensual and concrete values. Building on this metaphor, Derrida tries to rediscover the particular, sensual dimension of European metaphysics erased in the process of "polishing" its concepts. Analyzed as a result of such erasure, metaphysics shows its rich, sensual fullness and loses all

claims to objectivity: metaphysics is a mythology. See Jacques Derrida, "White Mythology," in *Margins of Philosophy*, trans. Alan Bass (Chicago: University of Chicago Press, 1982).

31. Spivak, *Post-Colonial Critic*, p. 144.

32. For an excellent analysis of the complexity of subject positions in subaltern cultures, see Gayatri Ch. Spivak, "Can the Subaltern Speak? Speculations on Widow-Sacrifice," *Wedge*, no. 7/8 (Winter–Spring 1985): pp. 120–130.

33. Homi Bhabha, "The Third Space," in Jonathan Rutherford, ed., *Identity: Community, Culture, Difference* (London: Lawrence and Wishart, 1990), pp. 207–221.

34. Hall, "Cultural Identity and Diaspora," p. 222.

35. See, for instance, Homi Bhabha, "The Commitment to Theory," *New Formations*, no. 5 (Summer 1988): pp. 5–23; Bhabha, "The Third Space."

36. Bhabha, "The Third Space," p. 210.

37. Mikhail Bakhtin, quoted in Lech Witkowski, *Uniwersalizm pogranicza: O semiotyce kultury Michala Bachtina w kontekscie edukacji* (Torun: Adam Marszalek, 1991), p. 106; my translation. Witkowski provides an extensive analysis of the educational implications of Bakhtin's work. In the American critical pedagogy this issue is taken up by Henry Giroux. See Giroux, *Schooling and the Struggle for Public Life*, pp. 117, 132–135, 199.

38. Bhabha, "The Third Space," p. 213.

39. Young, *White Mythologies*.

40. Abigail Solomon-Godeau, *Photography at the Dock: Essays on Photographic History, Institutions, and Practices* (Minneapolis: University of Minnesota Press, 1991), p. 209.

41. Paul Willis, *Learning to Labor: How Working Class Kids Get Working Class Jobs* (New York: Columbia University Press, 1984).

42. On the analysis of resistance, see Giroux, "Theories of Reproduction and Resistance in the New Sociology of Education," pp. 282–293; *Theory and Resistance in Education*, section 2.

43. Douglas Kellner, "Reading Images Critically: Toward a Postmodern Pedagogy," in Henry A. Giroux, ed., *Postmodernism, Feminism, and Cultural Politics: Redrawing Educational Boundaries* (Albany: State University of New York Press, 1991), p. 68.

44. Foucault, "Political Technology of Individuals."

45. Peter McLaren's work is important on the issue of the body in educational practices. See, for instance, *Schooling as a Ritual Performance*.

46. See Grossberg, "Teaching the Popular."

47. Of course there are significant differences between the United States and European countries in their health politics. This does not change the fact, however, that the United States also has a politics of health, one based on the notions of choice, competition, private ownership, and so on. This organization is claimed to provide the best health service for the population. There is no suggestion that the problem of health care does not concern the state.

48. Foucault, *Power/Knowledge*, pp. 97–98. Foucault coined a powerful phrase stating that subjectivity is formed as a result of subjection, and therefore it carries on power relations that gave it a shape. What I am attempting to do is to limit this notion to certain dimensions of subjectivity—those informed, or rather identified, by language or other cultural codes. Therefore it is identity rather than subjectivity that carries on relations of power. Of course, this discussion poses the question of definitions: what exactly is subjectivity, what is identity? I will not try to define these terms; I will be content with expressing the intuition that subjectivity is a broader term and refers to experiences that do not have to be conscious, identified by the subject, but that can remain in the "shadow" of nonverbalized and therefore unconceptualized emotions, desires, and so on. However, it seems that culture provides for possibilities of using emotions and affects as well in the role of "identifiers," of signs of identity, but this process implies also a kind of paralinguistic structuralization. For instance, pleasure can be conditioned in relations with cultural images. Here I am referring to processes of affective investments in identity construction, as analyzed by Grossberg. See, for example, Lawrence Grossberg, *We Gotta Get Out of This Place: Popular Conservatism and Postmodern Culture* (New York: Routledge, 1992).

49. Jonathan Rutherford, "A Place Called Home," in Jonathan Rutherford, ed., *Identity: Community, Culture, Difference* (London: Lawrence and Wishart, 1990), pp. 21–22.

50. See, for example, Peter McLaren's research into rituals of resistance in *Schooling as a Ritual Performance*.

51. Satya P. Mohanty, "Radical Teaching, Radical Theory: The Ambiguous Politics of Meaning," in Cary Nelson, ed., *Theory in the Classroom* (Urbana: University of Illinois Press, 1986), pp. 154–155.

52. Sarup, *Introductory Guide to Post-structuralism and Postmodernism*, p. 23.

53. Willis, *Learning to Labor*.

54. Bhabha, "The Third Space," pp. 212–213; Young, *White Mythologies,* p. 16.

55. Scholes, *Textual Power*, p. 62.

Chapter Three

Freedom and Postmodern Education

Pedagogical reactions to the postmodern situation—to the decentration of culture, the informational revolution, the new role of the media, and new social and political dynamics—can be interpreted in terms of freedom presupposed in their general, philosophical foundations, as well as in particular curricular projects. This concerns not just radical, emancipatory pedagogies with their direct liberatory claims. Education, in a way, has always been "about" freedom, and this tradition is visible in all contemporary tendencies. The question is, though, what freedom is at stake. However, the reason why I want to deal with a broader perspective than the one involving just the emancipatory pedagogy is not merely that it is possible; my intention is to sketch out a "map" of the concepts of freedom implied in the educational thinking of postmodernity, not just in those pedagogies that identify themselves with this cultural phenomenon, but also, to some extent, in those that try to oppose it. Only then will it be possible to understand the specificity of the radical approach to postmodern education.

It is often feared that the demise of grand narratives of modernity has induced a dangerous eruption of nihilism, hiding its threatening despair behind superficial relativism and indifference. Allan Bloom's provocative book is a classic example of this fear, as well as of a peculiar way of coping with it by means of total negation of the contemporary, by an escape to the idealized past of Platonic order.[1] Sometimes the very same process is considered to be the last major work of European Reason, liberating itself from itself, as Michel Foucault ironically formulated the condition for Reason to perform an emancipatory function.[2] Liberation from the grand narrative of Reason, however, puts into question the idea of progress, hopes for social change and a better future, and a sense of political action. Consequently, it seriously challenges the hope for freedom.

It is in this context that emancipatory pedagogy has to be analyzed in terms of its claims to freedom. These claims have to be treated as problematic and difficult, challenging the basic assumptions on which the whole emancipatory tradition of education has been built. Postmodern openness is considered to create emancipatory possibilities, and at the same time postmodernism challenges the notion of freedom conceived as autonomy and undercuts the notion of knowledge as a liberatory power. Freedom, crucial to the whole radical project of education, can no longer be conceived in rational and liberal terms, and there are hardly any other possibilities handy for its reformulation. They have to be carefully searched for or simply created. However, it is not the case that the educational project of postmodernity is dubious because its foundations are unstable. That project is founded upon a set of assumptions challenging the idea of foundations itself. Therefore, paradoxically, the final results of the theoretical project of pedagogy can be legitimately considered as a challenge to the foundations on which they have been based. This kind of inversion is truly postmodern itself; the outcome, the surface, the contingent, and the socially grounded are eventually more important than the ideal, the general, and the abstract and universal. Pedagogical consequences of philosophical analyses, probably for the first time in the history of educational theorizing, are more important than their philosophical foundations. They challenge these foundations; they compel their reformulation. The social and political anchorage of educational thinking, in other words, creates a unique position of critique and enables a possibility of questioning theoretical ideas, of interrogating them from an extratextual standing. Let me stress again that the project of critical pedagogy is theoretically problematic, and this is why it is so powerful and fascinating.

Pedagogies that try to return to great narratives of the past, to the canons of Great Books, or to various fundamentalisms as a remedy for the disquieting postmodern openness seem to have no theoretical problems whatsoever. They seek consolation in permanent closures of certainty and security stemming from clear-cut hierarchies of authority. There are other pedagogies that are oriented toward a traditionally liberal notion of freedom and toward tolerance of individual and cultural diversity. Still others take their inspiration from new horizons of scientific thinking, and in science they see the most powerful force capable of overcoming the heritage of positivism and modernist myths of Reason. There are also postmodern pedagogies that claim that it is time we forgot our past with its logocentric notions of freedom, individuality, reason, and progress, which were all produced by the culture of print, and started developing new literacies crucial for the new times of electronic media, the times that have already come. All these educational orientations make some direct or indirect references to the problem of freedom. They all address issues discussed in postmodern philosophy. Do they have anything in common? Are they totally dispersed, or is there a logic (or a paralogic) in their diversity? What are the differences behind that diversity?

WITHIN THE MODERN TRADITION: CHOICE AND IDENTITY IN CONSERVATIVE AND LIBERAL PEDAGOGIES

Although significant differences between conservative and liberal projects in education concern many issues, those concerning the notion of freedom do not seem to be deep. In both these traditions freedom is conceived as freedom of choice, and in both of them it is grounded in the autonomy of the subject. What they differ about, however, is the idea of subject. This difference stems from the way the conservative and liberal pedagogies ground their projects in broader notions of culture and humanity. Conservative projects tend to stress the hierarchical notion of culture, clearly distinguishing between "high" and "low" cultures and grounding educational goals in "high" cultural values. The process of education and development is portrayed as ascension toward higher and higher levels of cultural competence. Men and women, according to that model, acquire their abilities to make responsible choices (that is, their freedom) by gradually approaching subsequent stages of development and levels of education. Therefore, in conservative projects of educational reform (like George Bush's *America 2000*)[3] freedom of choice is ascribed to parents rather than to students. It is parents who can decide, according to their values and abilities, what school to choose for their children. Schools, too (or rather their managers) are treated as subjects of free choice in a particular, mercantile meaning of the word. They can "choose" to be good ones (academically oriented, skill-oriented, demanding, effective, and so on), or to be "bad" ones and to be doomed to failure. The rest is up to the market, good schools will survive and grow, bad ones will die.

This idea of an "educational market," apart from being dubious in terms of justice and equity, and sometimes ridiculous, if not dangerous, in its "Star Wars" approach to world politics (America as "the Power of Good"), seems also to be contradictory, which is a result of its fundamental assumptions. The typically conservative stress on cultural transmission, reinforced by the panic about the competitiveness of the American economy, makes the authors of *America 2000* introduce measurable criteria of school quality. Achievement tests are to cover all school subjects important in terms of their cultural canonicity and economic effectiveness. The contradiction in question can be seen in the strange idea of schools and students who can (that is, are free to) show their competencies in national tests serving the role of school assessment and valuation tools. This is choice with the results controlled administratively.

Schools and students can choose to be assessed, which is required in order to be considered "good" schools and students. This ambiguity seems to well reflect the logic of corporate capitalism and is twin-similar to the ambiguity of consumer choices analyzed by Bauman. It is a way of choosing that does not make a difference, that does not influence anything that could affect the general structure of social order.

America 2000 is not about the promotion of freedom, it is about effectiveness, and a strictly controlled one, concerning particular aspects of social life defined by the administration. It is almost desperate in its attempt to bureaucratically restore the extinct relation between individualism (linked to the freedom of choice) and the effectiveness of centralized power. *America 2000* is about power, about the ability to control the local and global political environment of the American economy. It is a strictly modernist project entangled in contradictions resulting from its inability to accept the postmodern (and thus postindustrial, postcolonial) world situation.

Liberal ideologies of education, traditionally concerned with individual development, tend to ground their visions rather in "natural" tendencies to self-actualization than in external factors. Hence, in classic articulations like the Rogersian one, the stress is on the child's freedom of choice, of decision making concerning the content and context of learning. Such visions of learning clearly oppose the notion of a gradation of responsible choices depending on the actual stage of development or level of education. As Colin Lankshear puts it, such an approach could be summed up as a postulate of education for freedom by means of deprivation of freedom.[4]

The liberal notion of freedom is also connected with a laissez-faire stress on tolerance. Everybody can choose what he or she wants, and as long as it is not dangerous to somebody else's life or freedom, it should be accepted. In present educational discussions in the United States we can clearly see that the stress on tolerance is the main concern within the liberal tradition, recently engaged in the question of multiculturalism. This pedagogy addresses the issue of Eurocentrism in American culture and the myth of the American melting pot, where all cultures were supposed to dissolve and merge into an American culture, losing their original identities. This myth, of course, is oppressive in racial and ethnic terms and is widely opposed by all minorities. In multicultural education the subject of freedom is both individualistic and collective: it is culture, cultural groups, and individuals who identify themselves with a given cultural milieu. The freedom here is not, however, a freedom of choice; rather, it is freedom to be the way one is, to construct and retain one's coherent cultural identity. What is it, then, that links this approach with the traditional liberalism, apart from the notion of tolerance and diversity?

The link seems to be, first of all, a particular silence concerning power and domination inscribed into relations between cultures and individuals. Such omissions, as a result, always serve the interests of the dominant power. In some articulations of multiculturalism, cultures appear not to influence one another; they "live side by side." They seem just to be diversities within a common culture,[5] diversities that, as Homi Bhabha says, hide the differences.[6] In some multicultural education projects one may sense an assumption that it is possible to know what particular cultures are "about," that one can limit their borders, preserve them in a "natural" shape, exhibit them as separate items of cultural diversity, and turn them into curricular subjects. This seems to be, as Gayatri Spivak makes clear, a new form of colonialism, a neocolonialism targeted on identity issues ("neocolonialism is identity talk").[7] Organizers of multicultural festivals in the United States, Spivak says, seem to know better what it means to be Indian than people of India, who have been fighting for their ethnic identities in bloody wars ravaging the subcontinent ever since the English left it.

The notion of culture in multicultural pedagogies seems to play the role informed by the notion of "nature" in liberal thinking. People are diversified; they come poor and rich, powerful and enslaved, but their basic nature is claimed to be the same. The right to freedom and the plea for tolerance are derived from that nature.

In multicultural pedagogies the role of human nature seems to be played by the notion of the "cultural nature" of identity. Our identities are defined by culture, and cultural differences make us diversified. Because all our beliefs are culturally informed, we apparently have no ground on which to base the judgement of those diversities. The right to freedom and the plea for tolerance are based on the recognition that all identities are cultural, and all claims to judge them are culturally biased. However, a particular danger appears here. It is one thing to say that identities are cultural, that they are built in culture, in relation to culture, or in relations between cultures, and another to claim that there is a "common culture," a fundamental sameness behind all differences. Such claims make multiculturalism look similar to the conservative educational projects, as it is very difficult, if possible at all, to define that "sameness" without referring to the ethnocentric assumptions of one's own culture. If we take into account the character of the contemporary relations between cultures, we may find out that the multiculturalism has its neo-colonial, Eurocentric dimension.

In spite of the ambiguity, the multicultural pedagogy is perhaps the most valuable outcome of liberal inspirations in the contemporary educational thinking. However, it is itself a "middle ground" on which a battle between contradictory tendencies is going on. The affirmation of differences, the discourse of the rights of all cultures to retain their identities, appear in this pedagogy next to conservative attempts at "ideological closures" of the multicultural flux. The modern opposition between the right to be different and cultural integrity is played again: this time, on the postmodern, multicultural ground.

NIHILISM AND HOLISM: EDUCATION BETWEEN DECONSTRUCTION AND THE NEW GNOSIS OF SCIENCE

The new image of science is one of the crucial aspects of the postmodern situation. Some theorists see contemporary science, quite paradoxically at the first view, as a major factor overcoming the modernist, positivist ideology of science that claims to be an ultimate solution to all the problems of humanity. Science itself, as some contemporary methodologists and scientists put it, is no longer positivistic. It has become aware of its own limitations, of its arbitrariness, and of the mythological foundations of its power. Its apparently neutral, objective discourse is grounded in narratives and self-justifying presumptions that cannot be interrogated within the positivist paradigm. Science, or rather scientism, the legitimizing ideology of science, is thus being questioned from within, from the perspective of its own assumptions. It makes this process congruent with deconstruction as described by Derrida. Deconstruction, again, appears to far exceed the realm of literary criticism. It rises to a major characteristic of contemporary thought interrogating itself.

In educational thinking Derridean inspirations have usually been separated from those derived from the new philosophy of science. The former influence the fields of literacy and politics; the latter mainly influence science education and, which may seem at odds with the stress on the particular and the different predominant in the postmodern culture, the holistic, ecological ethics of the New Age. However, their results do have something in common. To say the least, they are all postmodern educational projects and therefore deserve attentive analysis in terms of possible links, similarities, common fields, common features, and differences. Their differences seem obvious at first, but may look different when we try to see them against the background of the (meta)theoretical positions and relations.

In the following section I will discuss two groups of projects directly grounded in Derridean inspirations: the idea of deconstructive teaching (the notion of deconstruction concerns critical analysis from within discursive systems, aimed at dismantling their dualistic oppositions mainly by means of "undecidables," categories that, although created by the structural oppositions of the system, cannot "fit" in it, as they are virtually nondualistic), and Gregory Ulmer's idea of "teletheory" or "applied grammatology," an educational project based on Derrida's general theory of writing. I will also discuss briefly some projects grounded in "new science's" postpositivist methodologies developed mainly on the basis of relativistic theories such as Einstein's general theory of relativity, quantum physics, and so on. There is some deep link between the "new gnosis" of such methodologies and the proposals of some researchers concerned with literary theory that points to often overlooked holistic and, in a way, monistic dimension of postmodernism and poststructuralism.[8] It is interesting that the stress on difference and particularity, and the "neognostic," holistic, mythological approach to reality, are both derivable from the work of Derrida. This definitely calls for a closer consideration. The relation between the particular and the general is of great importance for all educational projects, and the tension (contradiction?) to which I am referring within basically the same body of theoretical knowledge is very promising in terms of illuminating this relation. Of course, my major concern will be with the notion of freedom presupposed in these projects, as well as within the field of their mutual relations.

In a text dealing with deconstructionist inspirations in literary education, Vincent Leitch presented a strategy of deconstructive teaching.[9] The first step in this process involves an "epistemological transformation," changing the attitude of the students to knowledge. What is at stake here is making them realize that knowledge is a "text" that has been written, has been created by somebody, and therefore is never absolute, but always partial and always open to criticism. On such a basis it is possible, in the second step, to stimulate the suspiciousness of the students, to make the structure of the text open to various partial interpretations, in short, to critically interrogate and transform the knowledge. The third step, very interesting, though rather controversial in terms of the pedagogical tradition, involves making the strategy of such teaching open to criticism as well. The basic rationale here is that this elaborated critical attitude to knowledge should not be confined to the texts analyzed in the classroom, but should address the very practice of the production of knowledge. Results of deconstructive teaching and learning should not be considered absolute. They must not replace old canons with a "new truth" of textual critique; that would merely produce another ideological closure and proclaim another universal doctrine. Leitch strongly argues against closing the heterogeneous, "undecidable" character of such critical practices within some defined political projects and positionings. That, he says, would deny the very nature of deconstruction:

> The politics of such "deconstructive teaching" moves beyond traditional liberal tolerance; it is usable with certain socialist, libertarian, and anarchic ideals. That this pedagogy could serve "right" or "left" political ideologies is, one would suppose, incriminating. Such heterogeneity or undecidability, however, is the hallmark of deconstructive productions. To purify such duplicity, to turn this new pedagogy toward a political doctrine or dogma, would be precisely to turn away from deconstruction, to end its teaching, which, nevertheless, is not apolitical, as Derrida makes clear.[10]

Such "political undecidability" is subject to criticism from various educational positions, especially within the body of critical pedagogy. As Henry Giroux and Peter McLaren argue, it merely serves the interests of dominant discourses of power, making the political character of textuality invisible and unquestionable.[11] Robert Scholes links this kind of "pure textuality" approach with narrow ways of reading structural and poststructural semiology, excluding the whole array of nonverbal signs from the process of communication. This makes it virtually impossible to transcend the limits of verbalization, to cross the border between the text and transtextual reality, and confines critical analyses and educational strategies to the "play of signifiers" that do not relate to anything but themselves. Scholes presents a pedagogical strategy that distinguishes between three levels of textual competence (textual power): reading, interpretation, and critique. All these levels of competence require active creation of texts. The process of reading depends on creating a text within the text. Interpretation requires creating a "metatext," a text upon the text. Critique is a process of creating a text against the text, and therefore it demands a clear extratextual positioning. The only possibility of critique is based upon social, political locations; it is grounded in the social experience. The strategy of deconstruction, argues Scholes, must be treated carefully so that it contributes to the textual power of the students and improves, not impairs, their ability to understand, interpret, and critically interrogate textuality.

A very interesting aspect of Scholes's proposal concerns a particular strategy of teaching for textual power, in a way opposing and at the same time supplementing the Derridean tradition of deconstruction. As Scholes argues, we can break dominant linguistic codes in two ways: we can either deconstruct them by applying a refined methodology of critique from within, based upon "undecidables" that break the signifying structure of the text, or we can create different codes, based on different structural relations, that break the dominant signifying structure by rupturing its order or charging its categories with different values. Scholes's analysis of Ursula Le Guin's novel *The Left Hand of Darkness* shows how this is possible. Le Guin describes an alien world inhabited by human-like beings who are hermaphrodites. The lack of sexual differences, or rather a pure contingency of these differences, deprives their culture of the dualism so predominant in our thinking. The title of the novel is a fragment of a poem that says that "light is the left hand of darkness" and "darkness is the right hand of light." In the structure of significations elaborated in the European tradition, as Scholes argues, exemplifying it with Aristotle's list of categories, "light" is positioned on the "right" side, "darkness" on the "left." To proclaim such structural relations contingent, as Le Guin does, challenges the deepest layers of our understanding. The encounter of our reading (facilitated by the presence of a human hero in the novel who tries to understand the alien culture) with such profound otherness makes the reader aware of deep, structural, linguistic limitations of understanding. Instead of deconstruction from within, here we have an encounter with an "extratextual," alternative location enabling critical distance from our own cultural codes. "The way of Le Guin," as Scholes calls this strategy, seems pedagogically at least equally as interesting as "the way of Derrida."[12]

Gregory Ulmer's theory is a very interesting attempt to implement Derrida's theory of writing—grammatology—in the construction of an educational practice relevant to the cultural breakthrough of postmodernity. The demise of logocentrism, of a philosophy (or rather of *the* philosophy, as the whole European tradition of metaphysics has been informed by this orientation) that positions the spoken word over the written, creates the notion of authenticity and direct accessibility of the world through the word, and erases the intermediated character of all representations, including oral and "purely" mental ones is one of the fundamental characteristics of postmodernity.[13] In Derrida writing is prior to speaking, as it is a model of the basic structure of signification resting on difference and deference. Meaning appears with a delay of representation, with substituting one thing for another. Such a notion opposes the metaphysical tradition based upon the premise of the priority of "directness" and therefore on the priority of speaking over writing. Speech, in that tradition, seems to be more directly linked to the "pure experience" grounded in language, in the word, in Logos perceived as directly linked to the nature of being. Writing seems then secondary, supplementary, unauthentic. But, as Derrida points out, any meaning must imply a kind of indirectness, a delay, a detour; difference, then, is constitutive to meaning. Writing, because its nature is based on substitution, on difference, is prior to speaking. Moreover, there is no meaning outside differences; therefore, meaning appears to be a constant play of signifiers that cannot be related to anything outside the text.

These notions have profound educational consequences, especially when we realize that the world of representations has replaced the "reality" in postmodern culture, and that it hardly represents anything external any longer. This phenomenon challenges traditional practices of education in the most direct way.

In his *Teletheory: Grammatology in the Age of Video*, Ulmer envisions a new body of educational practices grounded in different cultural competencies.[14] The culture of print is giving way to the culture of video, of visual presentations. Visual presentations are those that create our subjectivities and shape the world. The analysis of the "apparatus of knowledge" related to printed and electronic media reveals the complex character of competencies linked to these ways of knowledge production. The apparatus of the culture of print involves more than just the medium of the printed word. With it go competencies to read the word, to understand, to think critically, which always require the ability to derive, to abstract the meaning from the medium. The apparatus of the culture of print produces a specific form of human subjectivity: the rational, autonomous subject. "The Book" is read individually, its content is idealized and objectified, and its understanding requires abstraction. The rational subject is, therefore, a creation of the culture of print. The crisis of that culture, the expansion of the culture of video, is at the same time the crisis of the rational, individual subject. This crisis is a part of a larger process challenging the whole of what we used to call the heritage of the West; democracy, society, freedom, and cultural values are all questioned, threatened in their secure positions of sanctities. That visual culture presents a fundamental challenge to that heritage is acutely recognized and feared by conservative critiques of postmodernity calling for a return to "Great Books" in educational practices.

Ulmer's position is that we should learn the visual culture instead of despising it. It is only by actively using its language that we can start to understand its meanings. Schools, therefore, should concentrate on developing visual literacy ("videocy") and mental competencies related to visual media ("oralysis"). Oralysis—an educated form of oral competencies, argues Ulmer—is writable in video techniques just as analysis is writable in an alphabet. Contemporary culture in some way returns to orality, to preliterate forms of thinking and understanding, and to preliterate forms of social life. The new visual culture is a step back to orality repressed by the culture of print. It opens up forgotten spaces of holistic, mythical understanding, where the public and the personal, the rational and the mystical, and the theoretical and the practical are no longer antagonistic.

An educational strategy proposed by Ulmer reflects that process of reintegrating the categories separated by the logocentric, dualistic culture. His idea of "mystory" integrates in one educational narrative elements of "history" ("his story," "her story"), personal experience ("my story"), and mystery, located in a concrete "scene of writing." In this way it is becoming possible to create messages that overcome the limits of logocentric narration. They can hardly be written or discussed in a traditional way, but they can be presented in a form of video; they can create a "filmable theory." This new style of thinking is already present in our culture. It is used, for instance, in creative thinking throughout the domain of science, where personal narratives of sense merge with abstract concepts and theorems. The development of electronic media brings about a unique opportunity to make the processes of creative thinking accessible to virtually everybody. In order to understand ourselves in this new cultural situation, however, we have to practice the visual language, to use it even though we do not understand its codes. There is no other way to figure out the meaning of a new language than through its active usage. Ulmer claims that this practice will result in a new classical period of cultural creativity comparable to those that took place after the popularization of writing in ancient Greece and of print in Renaissance Europe.

Theoretical holism (overcoming the separation of rational and irrational ways of thinking, private and public knowledge, and other dualisms), and clear references to the new situation in the natural sciences as they become open to previously "unthinkable" strategies of inquiry questioning the basic assumptions of positivist methodologies, make Ulmer's proposal similar to some projects of science education. Educationists who accept the postmodern image of contemporary science express hope that the new science can help to overcome the relics of the culture of "grand narratives" since that culture was generally legitimized by the myth of objective, scientific truth.[15]

Postulates to make "new science" the basis for education usually address its probabilistic vision of reality, holism, teleology as opposed to traditional determinism, and hierarchism as an expression of discontinuity, of the multilayeredness of the world. They refer to the theses on the lack of balance, disequilibrium, as a basis for change through crises, replacing traditional concepts of evolutionary changes driven by mechanisms of adaptation and homeostasis.[16] In curriculum projects such assumptions call for structural openness and contradict the traditional rigidity that follows the spirit of Newtonian mechanics. Some theorists postulate the need of overcoming the postmodern fragmentation, which they consider a transitory phenomenon related to the end of the old social, political, and mental order not yet replaced by new unifying ideas, and they claim that this objective may be realized through education popularizing the holistic worldview of the new science, leading to new cultural consciousness. New science is here thought to be a transgressive medium of spirituality replacing the exhausted rationality. Education is conceived as a transgression from corporality through rationality to spirituality integrating the body and the mind.[17] This new spirituality, often referred to as the new gnosis, speaks to a different relation to the world, which has been elaborated, as Noel Gough says, in the feminist philosophy, which strongly opposes the "male," rational, exploiting attitude to the world, and in "green" ecopolitics.[18]

Deconstructive teaching, Ulmer's "teletheory," and the pedagogy of the new science occupy some common space in postmodern educational theorizing. How do they relate one to another? Where can we look for categories that make it possible to draw the boundaries of that common space? What kind of freedom can be defined within it?

Deconstructive teaching is liberatory. It suspends all discourses subjected to its strategy; moreover, it suspends itself. It exemplifies the Derridean "double gesture" of enunciation and cancellation, of erasure and keeping the sign visible under the erasure. It creates an empty space; it opens up the very form of signification that is empty, free from any meaning. In order to deal with the problem of meaning, Derrida says, "It is necessary in such a space . . . that writing literally means nothing. . . . It simply tempts itself, tenders itself, attempts to keep itself at the point of exhaustion of meaning."[19] In this context deconstructive teaching seems to be something like the concluding phase of the "didactics of Reason," of the didactic formalism linked to the rationalist epistemology. It is as if Reason really were to free us from itself through deconstruction.

The pedagogy of deconstruction is disquieting; it almost seems aimless. It engages and develops most refined competencies of critical thinking only not to allow anybody to make any meaningful use of them, apart from interrogating subsequent temporary conclusions, subsequent temptations to say "I know." That entire project would seem vain and futile, had it not been linked to some broader (philosophical, pedagogical, cultural, political) perspective. I will try to argue that this is the case, that the pedagogy of deconstruction is part of a larger, meaningful whole, or at least that it can be understood that way.

It is intriguing that the pedagogy of deconstruction appears to be an autonomous phenomenon of literary education, separated from other theoretical orientations, whereas the philosophy in which it is grounded is providing inspirations for virtually constructive projects, like the one proposed by Ulmer. If we are to investigate the problem of freedom in these pedagogies, we should therefore turn to Derrida himself. The apparent discrepancy in pedagogical readings of his work suggests that there may exist a broader perspective in which to think about postmodern education, one enabling us to see the aforementioned educational applications as particular projects dealing with separated aspects of the contemporary culture rather than representing its whole complexity.

Considering his own project of grammatology, Derrida, in a conversation with Henri Ronse, refers to the openness to nihilism, to a no-meaning I have already been talking about. As the search for the "meaning of meaning" is one of his basic concerns, Derrida has to take a position from which meaning can be observed in the process of its emergence, in its becoming. Such a position demands that writing be kept in a state of "no-meaning," on the verge of its exhaustion, in a space of dissemination of significations, of play of differences. This is not a transgressive position; it is not a position outside the language, above the meaning. "One is never installed within transgression, one never lives elsewhere."[20] The lack of meaning, the positioning within the space of exhausted, free, disseminating, playful meaning, is a position within the language, but this way of thinking does not imply an opposition between inside and outside, within and without. Therefore one can deconstruct the language, criticize it as if from outside while staying inside, using the language as the instrument of its own deconstruction. Thinking about meaning does not have a "real" outside; there is no metalanguage to criticize the language. "The thought-that-means-nothing, the thought that exceeds meaning and meaning-as-hearing-oneself-speak by interrogating them— this thought, announced in grammatology, is given precisely as the thought for which there is no sure opposition between outside and inside."[21]

Let us note that such unitariness, arriving in Derrida through the discussion on language and meaning, is a characteristic of all holistic philosophies, including the deterministic ones. This one feature seems already to point to a kind of coherence between deconstructive and holistic thinking in contemporary culture and seems to contribute to the belief sometimes expressed that the postmodern is a monistic philosophy.[22]

Writing philosophy that attempts to keep the writing within the sphere of the play of differences makes it possible for Derrida to critically investigate the Heideggerian opposition between beings (expressed as nouns, as "some-things that are") and Being (a verb, a fundamental process in which beings, secondary in nature, appear, shaped in oppositional structures). In Heidegger, the only access to the phenomenology of Being is through our "unauthentic" engagement in beings, or, more precisely, through our understanding of the unauthenticity of beings. It is only then that the sphere of Being does open up: Being "shines forth" through beings. In Derrida's interpretation this way of approaching the Being shows that there is a more fundamental, earlier rule that is prior to Being itself: the *différance* that makes it possible for the Being to exist in the form of beings. "Since Being has never had a 'meaning,' has never been thought or said as such, except by dissimulating itself in beings, then *différance*, in a certain and a very strange way, (is) 'older' than the ontological difference or that the truth of Being."[23] Being is preceded by difference, deference, detour; in order to be, "one" has to be different.

Derrida's is, then, a metaphysical project. It is a particular continuation of the search for the first rule, a continuation of the way in which Heidegger's opposition of Being as a process and particular beings seemed to be the last conceivable step. Some fragments of Derrida's writing show the gnostic character of this endeavor. Nothingness as "the meaning of meaning," the lack of opposition between the inside and the outside, the revelation of a rule prior to Being itself (a rule that cannot be named in ordinary language; (hence *différance*, combining notions of difference, deferring, detour), and an attempt to overcome the heritage of Heidegger, who himself is regarded as one of leading philosophers of the "new gnosis,"[24] are more than enough points to examine in Derrida's writing in the context of gnostic inspirations.

Contemporary gnosis is understood as nondualistic knowledge (overcoming the opposition of the subjective and the objective, of the inside and the outside, and so on) whose meaning rests rather with transforming the subject than explaining the object (hence psychoanalysis, for example, Jungian psychoanalysis, is regarded as gnostic in that aspect) and with exhausting itself in the very process of inquiry, on the way to knowledge rather than in final results of investigations. It is also a kind of knowledge that concerns "spiritual" aspects of reality, linking men and women with the world, and does not necessarily have a traditionally religious meaning; general systems theory or quantum physics are examples of such thinking. Spirituality is here conceived rather as a relation, a dimension of the process of understanding (as in Heidegger—understanding is a structure comprising the subject and the being, is Being-in-the-World itself). As Roberts Avens says, "We 'have' and we 'know' soul only on our way toward soul. Gnosis, like depth psychology, is soul-making."[25] "Soul" is here a rule of the subjectivity and of the world, "in which" rather than "with which" we live. The similarity of this notion to Heideggerian Being (*Dasein*) is clearly visible.

This approach to knowledge is often identified as characteristic of contemporary science shaped by revolutionary ruptures of twentieth-century physics. It is also visible in educational projects grounded in the "new science" approach I referred to earlier; the same seems to concern Gregory Ulmer's "teletheory," which clearly addresses the sphere of "the imaginary," crucial to the neognostic reconstructions of science.

If there is a notion of freedom implied in these pedagogies, it definitely is not grounded either in an individual subject or in the objective world. None of these ontological spheres exists separately in the philosophy that can be read behind them. The subject and the world appear to be separate entities, but their existence is "younger" than the ontological unity of Being-in-the-World and than the rule of *différance* prior to the one of Being. The separateness of the human being and the world, of the subject and the object, like any separateness, is created in language. It is only in that "constructedness," in the linguistically produced separateness, that we can talk about the autonomy of the subject; such autonomy is not, however, a kind of freedom that we could identify with the pedagogies discussed here. The autonomous, ontological subject in these pedagogies is subject to deconstruction, not to affirmation—as it is in ideas of deconstructive teaching and in Ulmer's "applied grammatology"—or is just "forgotten," erased, dissolved in a holistically conceived world, as it is in the ecopolitical pedagogy related to the "new science."[26]

If we agree that the function of gnostic knowledge is to transform the subject, we may say that in these pedagogies its meaning relies on freeing the subject from affective and cognitive "investments" into himself or herself, into a worldview, into particular objects and objectivity: freeing the subject from ideologies that freeze the flux of becoming into rigid and separated forms. Such a process seems to be oriented toward individual as well as cultural and social transformation (we can see it, for instance, in the postulates of ecological ethics that do not antagonize people and the world of nature). It is a pedagogy of liberation from the categorizing function of the language, from the "dogma of the noun." What is important, a pedagogy of this kind must be grounded in language itself; it is a form of critique that must include the criticized text. Knowledge is necessary for the process of freeing from knowledge; language is necessary to free ourselves from the language.

How can we, then, grasp such a notion of freedom? I think that turning once again to Heidegger may be of some help here. In his lectures on Schelling's treatise on freedom Heidegger wrote: "Freedom is here not a property of man, but the other way round: man is at best the property of freedom. Freedom is the encompassing and penetrating nature, in which man becomes man only when he is anchored there. That means the nature of man is grounded in freedom." Freedom, therefore, is conceived not as an "addition and attribute of the human will, but rather as the nature of true Being, as the nature of the ground for beings as a whole."[27]

Let us note that this ontological vision does not erase individual freedom: it just places it as a secondary phenomenon, as an effect of metaphysical (linguistic, logocentric) construction. The interrogation of this construction—and with it, of the whole metaphysical, Eurocentric tradition, of the "white mythology," deconstructs the ontological subject—deconstructs, which means discovers the rules of its linguistic construction.[28] The subject, deprived of its grounding in a dualistically ideologized world, deconstructed, decentered, becomes a hybrid, an unfulfilled identity constantly "under construction" in relation to languages, ideologies, and discourses of power.

The pedagogy of deconstruction, Ulmer's "teletheory," and the pedagogy of "new science" do not concentrate directly on social contexts of education. Their references to ideology (understood as the discursive practice of identity construction), to culture (an opposition of literary "analysis" and visual "oralysis" that opens up new possibilities of identity construction in Ulmer's theory), and to scientific knowledge (as unifying with the world, reinscribing people into the dynamics of Cosmos in the pedagogy of "new science") tend to overlook the institutional dimension of discursive practices and to set aside political aspects and relations of power deciding on the validity of particular forms of knowledge. Such an attitude is being criticized. Michael Ryan says that deconstruction, as reconstruction of reason, must take into account the institution where reason is "produced and transmitted," that is education.[29] Henry Giroux and Peter McLaren challenge the deconstructive pedagogy for its practice of undermining the "viability of political work by enacting the discourse of profound skepticism," as well as for its "overall lack of public philosophy, its lack of organic connections to a wider public sphere, its suffocating emphasis on a narrow notion of textuality, its domination by intellectuals from elite schools, and its almost unreadable pedanticism [that] makes it less a threat to the established configurations of power than an unwilling ally."[30]

I think, however, that this apolitical educational movement may have some political meaning (see Derrida's notion of the indirect politicity of deconstruction), although not directly.[31] Deconstruction of the subject opens up theoretical possibilities of overcoming adaptive visions of identity formation and their one-dimensional determinism and leads toward a possibility of analyzing the hybrid dimension of subjectivity, which can be a point of reference in constructing the ethical discourse of education. This way of thinking about subjectivity—subjectivity after deconstruction—makes it possible to address the problems of the transformation of the political subject of education.

BEYOND INDIVIDUALISM: FREEDOM IN CRITICAL PEDAGOGY

One may say that in the background of critical pedagogy there is the negative, liberal notion of individual freedom, or more precisely an awareness, to say the least, of the impossibility of the liberal project. Individuals do not live in a vacuum, nor can they isolate themselves from numerous relations of dependence. The space of their lives is filled with relations that are neither symmetric nor based on equal exchange. These relations are more or less institutionalized, are permeated with power, and comprise domination and subjugation. The organizational structure of societies is aimed at reproducing these relations, which makes the whole liberal project either utopian or turns it into a cynical ideology that sustains the privilege of freedom for some, for those few who can control conditions of their lives. With the category of reproduction, there arrives in educational discourse a postulate of emancipation, of freeing people from social, economic, and political oppression. The project of emancipation becomes more and more refined when educational theory adopts contemporary theories of power. But with the openness to poststructural notions of decentered power dissolved in social relations, permeating the very tissue of everyday life, grounded in the medium, most common and impossible to overcome, of language, the project of emancipation faces the challenge of nihilistic hopelessness. If power is in language, if it soaks into everyday social relations, if it is enfleshed into people's bodies, the postulate of emancipation may sound like a cry for war against everything.

But the notion of freedom in critical pedagogy is not merely negative. It is not limited to the idea of emancipation bringing about a "freedom from everything." The idea of emancipation has always been accompanied by the idea of empowerment. The concept of empowerment is clearly grounded in values and in the "positive" tradition of the philosophy of freedom. This interrelation of negative and positive freedom, of emancipation and empowerment, seems crucial for the project of critical pedagogy. In critical pedagogy, empowerment refers to supra-individual dimensions of education. It speaks to postulates of creating another, more just and more direct form of democracy that could bring about a broadening of the scope of freedom for groups and individuals.

The project of democracy, however, is strictly related to issues of individuality, of subject formation in the process of education. The subject of education is neither merely collective nor individual; it is a postmodern subject within which social, cultural, and political processes create a sphere of conflict and negotiation. Stanley Aronowitz and Henry Giroux are worth quoting at length on this issue:

No longer viewed as merely the repository of consciousness and creativity, the self is constructed as a terrain of conflict and struggle, and subjectivity is seen as the site of both liberation and subjugation. How subjectivity relates to issues of identity, intentionality, and desire, is a deeply political issue that is inextricably related to social and cultural forces that extend far beyond the self-consciousness of the so-called humanist subject.[32]

As the theoretical perspective of postcolonialism seems to suggest, the multidimensional, hybrid identity can be conceived, by itself and by others, in the form of a "humanist," ontological subject (that is, a subject who is positioned against an object, differentiating himself or herself from the Other) only as a result and to the extent of ideological closures within dualistic, metaphysical structures, in linguistic constructs based upon oppositions characteristic of conceptual categorizations. Such a perception of subjectivity as a unified subject is dialectically intertwined with the hybrid openness. The dialectic character of subjectivity seems to stem on the one hand from the desire of clarity, of closure (hybridity is problematic; one needs an identity, some positioning, a location from which to speak, and this is possible, for instance, when one enters a community and develops a notion of solidarity), and on the other from the inevitable temporality and provisionality of closures and identifications.

The dialectics of openness (hybridity, nonsovereignty) and closure (ontological autonomy, the self opposed to the Other) are strictly connected to the dialectics of freedom in relation to power.

The "closed," individual freedom, setting the self against the Other (this kind of freedom seems to be constructed as a result of "coping" with power relations in the process of identity formation) is in a dialectic relation with "another" freedom, relational freedom overcoming the opposition of the individual and the social, of the negative and the positive, freedom as the grounding for humanity rather than its feature, freedom of Being in the Heideggerian sense. Let us note Henry Giroux's analysis of the notion of empowerment:

> This notion has a double reference: to the individual and to society. The freedom and human capacities of individuals must be developed to their maximum but individual powers must be linked to democracy in the sense that social betterment must be the necessary consequence of individual flourishing. Radical educators look upon schools as social forms. Those forms should educate the capacities people have to think, to act, to be subjects, and to be able to understand the limits of their ideological commitments. That's a radical paradigm. Radical educators believe that the relationship between social forms and social capacities is such that human capacities get educated to the point of calling into question the forms themselves. What the dominant educational philosophies want is to educate people to adapt to those social forms rather than critically interrogate them. Democracy is a celebration of difference, the politics of difference, I call it, and the dominant philosophies fear this.[33]

We can see here a unity of the project of individual empowerment and social development; we can see power relations grounded in life forms that can be interrogated and changed as long as human capacities of critical thinking and acting are developed, not blocked, in the process of education; we can see the notion of democracy as the politics of difference. All these dynamics of social development can be frozen in limiting forms, fixed as "given," as "the heritage of the past," as "the best of all possible worlds." Such are the desires of the conservative mind driven by the fear of "unlabelling," of lack of names, of the flux of becoming and of the openness of Being. To make things more complicated, that desire is inevitable. Ideological closure of social life forms is a kind of "impossible necessity." As Ernesto Laclau points out, to the postmodern consciousness society appears as something impossible, deprived of grounding in any stable base, shaky and constantly threatened in its cohesion. In interpersonal relations the existence of society, as a background of these relations, is a necessity. The role of creating and maintaining the social, therefore, must be played by ideology. Ideology is a form of linguistic articulation, a conceptual closure of what is basically non-conceptualizable, liquid, and amorphous. In this sense utopia, an ideological articulation of nonexisting society, is a necessary cohesive element of human agency.[34] The thing is, however, that institutionalized ideology incorporated into language, schooling, politics, and so on must be open to interrogation, must be subject to critique and, when necessary, to rejection. It must be a discursive practice, not an institution of totalitarian power. In order to be so, education must provide for (maintain, re-create, or simply create) public spheres, spheres of discursive articulation, critique, and "social dreaming," to borrow the term from Peter McLaren.[35]

We are approaching here a crucial aspect of understanding the notion of freedom in postmodern radical pedagogy, in the simplest way grasped by Giroux and Simon as "understanding of necessity and transformation of necessity."[36] The task of this pedagogy is not simply to liberate people; as I have tried to show, the dynamics of identity formation in relation to power make it possible to create individual spheres of freedom, both negative (which can be attained in acts of mimicry hiding an individual from the gaze of power) and positive (emulation is clearly oriented toward enhancing individual control over the environment through the attainment of attributes of higher social status). The hybridity that inevitably results from these endeavors, as well as from acts of resistance, is from the perspective of the needs of "identity under construction" a particular disaster, a constant unfulfillment. But it is just the hybridity, the nonsovereignty, the amorphousness of the subject that, as I understand it, is the referent of educational projects in critical pedagogy. Individual freedom, the autonomy of the subject, is not celebrated by radical pedagogy. On the contrary, as Henry Giroux points out in numerous writings, being the point of departure of educational projects, it should be interrogated. The particular subject position, as a place of enunciation of the "voice" of the student must be reaffirmed as a condition of emancipatory articulation, but also questioned in terms of its relations to other voices, of its place in the sphere of public life. Identities constructed in relation to power carry with them some aspects of domination they tried to cope with or resist in their histories. If education is to question domination, it has to interrogate people's voices, along with conceptually protected, closed, inaccessible spheres of individual freedom elaborated in individual relations to the structures of power. Thus individuals are challenged to question their autonomy, to accept their own uncertainty, openness, hybridity, and vulnerability, and to turn to others not with cognitive intentions to frame, conceptualize, and close, to appropriate the other and thus demarcate the border of the self, and to conceptualize one's own self-consciousness as separate from the Other, but in the gesture of solidarity, in an ethical relation opening up the perspective of *communitas*. Solidarity and participation in the public sphere, in *communitas*, make it possible for individuals to position themselves within particular dynamics of social relations, political goals, and struggles, to identify themselves with these positions, and to take up the question of political freedom.

Linguistic, discursive practices and power relations claiming their rights to shape people's identities are challenged from two perspectives: from "below," from the level of the body, from affects and desires, and generally from the pretextual, imaginary experience providing ground for an individual to enter relations of power not merely as an object of formative discursive forces, but as an agent who can, to some extent, shape these relations, winning some scope of individual freedom (however prescribed that freedom may be); and from "above," from the perspective of extratextual social practices that are the site of articulation, of the creation of discourses. To enter that second perspective, one has to be open in his or her hybridity, the nonsovereignty resulting from individual struggles for freedom. Solidarity, *communitas*, and public spheres of articulation can provide a location for counterdiscourses, for the creation of "texts against the (dominant) text," and for critique, and the foundation for a noninclusive democracy of differences.

Democracy grounded in the nonsovereign subject, as Homi Bhabha maintains, has a chance to avoid the danger of cultural oppression, of the appropriation of differences into a mystified sphere of cultural diversity. Democracy, however, is a very fragile project, demanding constant, active, and critical support. It is very easy to slip into the need for ideological certainty, where the power to define, to name, would be entrusted to someone playing the role of mythical father. Democracy is a project that survives on the verge of totalitarianism. What keeps it from slipping into the certainty of totalitarianism is constant dissatisfaction with institutionalized power, the constant impotence, proven again and again, of succeeding authorities. Dissatisfaction of this kind protects us from believing in the powers of any individual to satisfy our needs of certainty and security, to define our identities and the identities of others; and thus dissatisfaction protects democracy. Joan Copjec says on this issue: "It is only dissatisfaction and this struggle over the definition of the subject and of its relations to other subjects that prevents us from surrendering this power of definition to the Other. It is only because I doubt that I am therefore a democratic citizen."[37] Once again, the openness of identity and critique are proclaimed basic factors of democracy, of political freedom.

In this kind of theoretical thinking, the postmodern vision of social life is challenged in two dimensions: first, the postmodern dispersion resulting from the rejection of master narratives, owing to which the very notion of society or any other coherent social structure is difficult to maintain; second, social determinism, paradoxically coexisting with the notion of the demise of society, visible in the role ascribed to power and language in the process of identity construction. Although both Foucault and Derrida have overcome deterministic features of structural inspirations in their theories (Foucault through the notion of resistance grounded in the multiplicity of determining discourses, Derrida through deconstruction of language), the applications of their thought in the social theory seem mainly to celebrate hopelessness resulting from the merciless acuteness of the analyses of power relations. Many social theorists who take up postmodern categories in their studies are aware of the necessity to challenge the intellectual framework of postmodernity, and they do this mainly through stressing some continuity between postmodernism and modern projects of enlightenment, democracy, and emancipation. In such a perspective postmodernism seems to be a shift between the center and the peripheries of culture rather than a rupture of its history. As a result, postmodernity, because of its openness and decentration, may enable the realization of some modernist ideals. As Ernesto Laclau argues, the demise of fundamental ideas of modernity may mean that chances of social emancipation are better than ever, because it is social groups, and not abstract rules of Reason, that are the source of the articulation of political ideas. The lack of foundations, the "horizontality" of postmodern culture, may therefore signify the beginning of the process of "global emancipation."[38] Stanley Aronowitz and Henry Giroux write on this issue:

The task of modernity, with its faith in reason and emancipation, can perhaps renew its urgency in a postmodern world, a world where difference, contingency, and power can reassert, redefine and in some instances collapse the monolithic boundaries of nationalism, sexism, racism, and class oppression. In a world whose borders have become chipped and porous, new challenges present themselves not only to educators but to all those to whom contingency and loss of certainty do not mean the inevitable triumph of nihilism and despair but rather a state of possibility in which destiny and hope can be snatched from the weakening grasp of modernity.[39]

Whether this will happen depends much on education.

DETERMINISM, SUBJECTIVITY, AND THE QUESTION OF FREEDOM: TOWARD A THEORETICAL CLOSURE OF EDUCATIONAL (POST)MODERNISM

When the foundations of the Newtonian cosmic order began to shake, the deterministic explanatory models "slid down" from Cosmos to the Earth, from the world of nature to the one of humanity and society. The notion of human nature—or natural, biological determinism in the social sciences—gave way to thinking in terms of the determining role of history, culture, and language. That shift was reflected also in the investigations into transcendency. Structural analysis of the myth is a kind of cultural theology; it creates knowledge on the linguistic, cultural, and structural foundations of religion and thus replaces metaphysical proofs of the existence of God. Characteristic of postmodernity, a horizontal space of understanding and explaining the world opens up, as if with the demise of hope for the Universal Clock to regulate the order of the Earth, humanistic thought had nothing more to look for in the worlds above people's heads. The world of nature, deprived of its features of "otherness," of deterministic rigidness, has stopped resisting the humanistic mind, has stopped providing a countermodel for what it means to be human. It no longer provides counterconcepts for "free will," "creativity," or "spirituality." Its contemporary reconstructions do not lend themselves to easy contradictions between naturalistic "explanations" and humanistic "understanding."

Can humanistic thought develop only in opposition to some nonhumanistic one? Can we speak about freedom only as opposed to determinism? Probably so. But grounding this opposition in a deterministically conceived social world proved to present a fundamental challenge to the humanities. Determinism grounded in social structures, in power relations permeating everyday life situations and soaking our bodies, in the language through which we attempt to define ourselves, challenged the very idea of human subjectivity. There came an openness that exceeded the border between the subject and the objective world; subjectivity began to vanish in a web of cultural and political relations.

The questioning of the idea of subjectivity, which by itself is difficult to come to terms with, presents a fundamental challenge to all spheres of social thought and practices referring to human activity, agency, and responsibility. Without a subject, or rather with a decentered subject deprived of clear identity, the grounding of all these categories is questionable. It is not only in abstract cultural values, but also in the sphere of individual experience and social practice that the challenge of nihilism has to be faced.

The attempt to present the process of identity formation in terms of relation to power rather than of power relations, undertaken in chapter 2, is an attempt to defer the problem of subjectivity, to create a space in which speaking of both power and agency will be possible, where along with discursively grounded subject positions one can imagine the body as one of these positions, the one from which to read and interrogate power relations and subject positions "offered" for identity construction. It is in this space that relational, hybrid identity is being formed: identity open to the social world, identity as a surface, a border sphere between the within and the outside. But what is "within"? It is not a rational center; it is not a conceptual structure of the "I." Perhaps it is just the biological, animal sensibility of a living creature, a basic openness to the environment, a two-way gate linking biological tissues with social relations. The "within" is not an ontological subject. Its human shape, its ontological being, is constructed in relations with social discourses. Its "definition" comes from the language.

Is a human being free? What is free in her, in him? What is the scope of freedom in that strangely conceived, physically open and socially closed being? If we wanted to ground human nature in the cosmic plan, according to the metaphysical tradition, the human microcosm would have to be imagined, in its deepest nature, as not determined. This is a paradoxical thesis: the nature of human being is the lack of nature. Or, in other words, its nature, if conceivable, is merely of formal character; it is empty, not defined. We can only construct theoretical visions of relations, transformations, and borders, without any content matter, without any possibility of stating the probability that such and such "substances" reside within the field of these relations. Mimicry, resistance, domination, or subjugation can all solve the problem of "location," can situate an individual within the field of social relations. All of them fill the same formal structure; they can occupy the same "empty" place of our existence in relation to the world, and all of them fit the place equally well. The difference between them is not of ontological nature; it is not determined by any "nature." It is shaped by culture, by language, by the ethics of social relations, by the agency of the subject trying to solve the problem of location.

Thus it is language that gives us identity, but language is no longer an emanation of Universal Reason, Logos identical with the nature of the world in which all possibilities of true cognition were hoped to be inscribed. Language is a human creation and is used by humans as an instrument of control: *command* is the most common use of language. To the extent that we have a command of language, we can articulate names and orders; we can have command over others and over the world. In relations of power, of control, of having command, and of being commanded, we elaborate our identities, we construct ourselves, at the same time constructing others.

As philosophers of postcolonialism maintain, European metaphysics is a philosophy of conquest. It is built upon philosophical allergy, on a lack of tolerance for the Other who dares to remain other. Within the structure of European mind the Other cannot be left like that; it must become an object (of my thought, my language, my command, my mastery), it must be appropriated into ready-to-use categorical structures, it must fall into a whole of some kind. Robert Young, in his account of Emmanuel Levinas's ideas, notes the relation between the notion of freedom and the process of appropriation of the Other. Levinas wrote: "Imperialism of the same is the whole essence of freedom," and Young explains: "For freedom is maintained by a self-possession which extends itself to anything that threatens its identity."[40] Personal freedom is thus gained and maintained by the subordination of others. This is, Young notes, a replica of the political situation in which European democracies were established upon the exploitation of non-European colonies.

Can we know the Other respecting his or her identity? Levinas claims that we can, if we manage to free ourselves from the "visual" metaphor of cognition. The metaphor of light, of vision, prevailing in European metaphysics throughout its history, from Plato to Heidegger, makes us believe that cognition is a form of "incorporation," of appropriation. That is the Greek tradition. European philosophy, however, has also a root in the Jewish tradition, and that is founded on the metaphor of dialogue, of listening and speaking. Dialogue is free from the characteristic of appropriation. In dialogue, language keeps partners apart, maintains distance between them, and provides for no opportunity of incorporation. Moreover, the structure of dialogue excludes a possibility of adopting a "third," external position where partners would be perceived as belonging to a greater whole. The relation in dialogue is, therefore, a relation of difference, of separation through speech.

As I have mentioned in chapter 2, the ontological subject, constructed on the basis of appropriation of otherness, adopting his or her position through "singling out," naming and labelling, and then reducing the Other to something he or she is not, is in Levinas's proposal replaced by the ethical subject. Let us quote Young again: "Levinas proposes the possibility that the much lamented 'subject' be brought back not as the ontological subject which seeks to reduce everything to itself but as an ethical subject defined in relation to the other. Ethics redefines subjectivity as this heteronomous responsibility in contrast to autonomous freedom."[41]

It seems that we have to do with a deep relationship between the process of deconstruction of the ontological subject and the attempts to ground subjectivity in the domain of ethics. Decomposition of the deterministic philosophy of nature on the one hand, and construction of deterministic philosophies of history, culture, and society on the other, opened up the possibilities, and created the demand, of reconstructing the subject in ethical relations with others, in the sphere of responsibility. In this postmodern perspective, freedom is rather a state of world than an attribute of an individual. A free man is free to the extent that somebody else is deprived of freedom (note Bauman's thesis on the relational nature of freedom), as a result of some compromise, some dialectic of struggle and complicity within the field defined by dominant power relations. Human freedom is thus confined to structures of domination; it is a "closure" in relation to these structures, which means that in order to overcome the structures of domination, one has to give up a scope of secure freedom guaranteed by them. This means that one has to be able to give up his or her defined, safe, stable, and well-known, identity, "ontologized" by linguistic labels. Such decentration of the ontological subject, its hybridity, its nonsovereignty (see Bhabha's theory), seems to provide for an opportunity of openness to the ethical, to responsibility and solidarity. Here appears the possibility of freeing the sphere of public life, of opening it to the process of change, of overcoming the structural determination inscribed into decentered relations of power.

In this context the pedagogies discussed earlier (deconstructive teaching, the "new science" approach, "teletheory" based on visual media and oral competencies, and radical/critical pedagogy) seem to be situated in a common metatheoretical space reflecting the cultural change of postmodernity. This does not mean, however, that these theories can be equated, that they are congruent or basically "the same"; on the contrary, they present a new array of tensions, conflicts, and oppositions. It is between them that theoretical discussions are sure to be most heated. Still, just as modernity was a project grounded in the discussion between subjectivism and objectivism, and its cultural identity was constructed between these positions, it seems plausible that the cultural epoch appearing before our very eyes in the yet cumbersome form of postmodernity will be defined by the struggle between "openness" and "closures" it will have to take up: the struggle between the nihilistic openness of ex-subjectivity, now tended to be fixed in its deconstructed flux, and new forms of social identity that overcome the opposition of the private and the public; the struggle between the culture of visuality, which can easily be turned into a most powerful medium of unification and appropriation, and ethical responsibility grounded in dialogue and difference. Postmodern pedagogies already seem to have started taking positions and making themselves ready for these struggles.

As long as deconstructive teaching seems to be an attempt at closing the project of modernity by leading critical thought to its (suicidal) end, other orientations try to make some use of the deconstruction of the ontological subject. The "new science" pedagogy tries to situate subjectivity in an ecological setting, in a relation to the Earth drawn so broadly that it makes any reference to autonomous (that is, traditionally free) individuality virtually impossible. The ecological human being is first of all responsible for the world, not free from the others. To make this responsibility a real factor of social life takes radical changes in the ways this life is organized, but this political issue is rarely taken up in the "neognostic" thinking of "new science" pedagogies. Gregory Ulmer's applied grammatology and teletheory, as well as some other educational projects related to the artistic avant-garde, make use of the deconstruction of linear, logocentric, "alphabetic" consciousness. Ulmer makes it clear that individual freedom is linked to logocentrism and alphabetical consciousness, and it is this link that makes conservatives react so strongly against postmodern culture. Ulmer argues, however, that it is not free individuals that make society possible. Visual/oral education, refining and redefining elements of premodern, oral, mythical culture, may be a strong premise on which to build new, different forms of social life, not necessarily worse than those based on the ideology of individual freedom, always presupposing some form of domination.

The project of critical pedagogy, here identified with its version presented by Henry Giroux and Peter McLaren, is in my opinion the most advanced, complex, and consequent vision of postmodern education, in a way including elements present in all previously discussed orientations, being at the same time not their synthesis or metatheory. It is a project of education that liberates, first of all, the sphere of public life, creating premises for education oriented toward solidarity and responsibility in *communitas*, in social structures open to democratic participation without isolating them in a way that could re-create colonial structures of "othering." This kind of education takes as its point of departure the hybridity, the nonsovereignty of the individual subject, and presents a vision of challenging individual autonomy where it is built upon exclusions, domination, and "othering," to an extent that makes it possible to create communities where new possibilities of human life can be opened up.

What, then, are emancipation, empowerment, and liberation in the discourse of postmodern education? In its elementary, material layer of biological life human nature seems not to be determined; to recall Heidegger, we may say that "man is in freedom"; it is an empty form to be filled with meaning. The meaning is acquired in social relations, in relations of power and control. It is there that human subjectivity is defined. The ontological identity thus acquired is laden with dramatic tension, is in constant conflict with defining social relations, and eventually forms itself as a nonsovereign hybrid. Emancipatory education seems to be aimed at freeing the human hybrid from the need of ideological closure, of being labelled, defined once for good. This kind of freedom enables liberation of the public, of *communitas*, for it is hybridity that opens us up to dialogical exchange that does not subjugate differences. Emancipatory education liberates the sphere of politics as a discursive practice, as an open area of articulation, of interrogating culture, ideology, and power; it therefore opens up the possibility of control over what defines human identities. This is where the political project of radical pedagogy touches the very issue of the nature of human being.

NOTES

1. Allan Bloom, *The Closing of the American Mind: How Higher Education Has Failed Democracy and Impoverished the Souls of Today's Students* (New York: Simon and Schuster, 1987). For comments on Bloom's work, see also note 25 to chapter 1.

2. See Robert Young, *White Mythologies: Writing History and the West* (London: Routledge, 1990), p. 9.

3. *America 2000: An Education Strategy* (Washington, D.C.: U.S. Department of Education, 1991).

4. Colin Lankshear, *Freedom and Education* (Auckland: Milton Brookes Publications, 1982), chapter 1.

5. See the critique of the notion of "common culture" in Diane Ravitch's project of education for cultural pluralism in Henry A. Giroux and David Trend, "Cultural Workers and the Pedagogy of Cultural Politics: Writing Against the Empire," in Henry A. Giroux, *Border Crossings: Cultural Workers and the Politics of Education* (New York: Routledge, 1992), pp. 234–236.

6. Homi Bhabha, "The Commitment to Theory," *New Formations*, no. 5 (Summer 1988): 18–19.

7. Gayatri Ch. Spivak, "Neocolonialism and the Secret Agent of Knowledge," *Oxford Literary Review* 13, no. 1/2 (1991): 234.

8. See, for example, Stephen Crook, "The End of Radical Social Theory? Radicalism, Modernism, and Postmodernism," in Roy Boyne and Ali Rattansi, eds., *Postmodernism and Society* (New York: St. Martin Press, 1990); Ihab Hassan, "The New Gnosticism: Speculations on an Aspect of the Postmodern Mind," in *Paracriticisms: Seven Speculations of the Times* (Urbana: University of Illinois Press, 1975).

9. Vincent Leitch, "Deconstruction as Pedagogy," in Cary Nelson, ed., *Theory in the Classroom* (Urbana: University of Illinois Press, 1986).

10. Ibid., p. 54.

11. Henry A. Giroux and Peter McLaren, "Language, Schooling, and Subjectivity: Beyond a Pedagogy of Reproduction and Resistance," in K. Borman, P. Swami, and L. Wagstaff, eds., *Contemporary Issues in*

U.S. Education (Norwood, N.J.: Ablex Publishing Corporation, 1991), pp. 76–77.

12. Robert Scholes, *Textual Power: Literary Theory and the Teaching of English* (New Haven, Conn.: Yale University Press, 1985).

13. Gregory Ulmer, *Applied Grammatology: Post(e)-Pedagogy from Jacques Derrida to Joseph Beuys* (Baltimore: Johns Hopkins University Press, 1985). On the demise of logocentrism, see, for example, Jacques Derrida, "The End of Book and the Beginning of Writing," in *Of Grammatology*, trans. by Gayatri Ch. Spivak (Baltimore: Johns Hopkins University Press, 1976).

14. Gregory Ulmer, *Teletheory: Grammatology in the Age of Video* (New York: Routledge, 1989).

15. Philip Wexler, "Curriculum in the Closed Society," in H. Giroux and P. McLaren, eds., *Critical Pedagogy, the State, and Cultural Struggle* (Albany: State University of New York Press, 1989), pp. 92–104.

16. William E. Doll, Jr., "Foundations for a Post-Modern Curriculum," *Journal of Curriculum Studies* 21, no. 3 (1989), pp. 243–253.

17. Richard A. Slaughter, "Cultural Reconstruction in the Postmodern World," *Journal of Curriculum Studies* 21, no. 3 (1989), pp. 255–269.

18. Noel Gough, "From Epistemology to Ecopolitics: Renewing the Paradigm for Curriculum," *Journal of Curriculum Studies* 21, no. 3 (1989): 225–241.

19. Jacques Derrida, "Implications: Interview with Henri Ronse," in *Positions*, trans. Alan Bass (Chicago: University of Chicago Press, 1981), p. 14.

20. Ibid., p. 12.

21. Ibid.

22. See, for example, Crook, "The End of Radical Social Theory?" p. 58.

23. Jacques Derrida, "Différance," in *Margins of Philosophy*, trans. Alan Bass (Chicago: University of Chicago Press, 1982), p. 22.

24. Roberts Avens, *The New Gnosis: Heidegger, Hillman, and Angels* (Dallas: Spring Publications, 1984).

25. Ibid., p. 7.

26. Gough, "From Epistemology to Ecopolitics."

27. Martin Heidegger, *Schelling's Treatise on the Essence of Human Freedom* (Athens: Ohio University Press, 1985), p. 9.

28. See Jacques Derrida, "Deconstruction and the Other," in Richard Kearney, *Dialogues with Contemporary Continental Thinkers: The Phenomenological Heritage* (Manchester, England: Manchester University Press, 1984).

29. Michael Ryan, *Marxism and Deconstruction: A Critical Articulation* (Baltimore: Johns Hopkins University Press, 1982).

30. Giroux and McLaren, "Language, Schooling, and Subjectivity," pp. 76–77.

31. Derrida, "Deconstruction and the Other."

32. Stanley Aronowitz and Henry A. Giroux, *Postmodern Education: Politics, Culture, and Social Criticism* (Minneapolis: University of Minnesota Press, 1991), p. 76.

33. Henry A. Giroux, *Border Crossings: Cultural Workers and the Politics of Education* (New York: Routledge, 1992), p. 11.

34. Ernesto Laclau, "The Impossibility of Society," in *New Reflections on the Revolution of Our Time* (London: Verso, 1990).

35. Peter McLaren, "Critical Pedagogy: Constructing an Arch of Social Dreaming and a Doorway to Hope," *Journal of Education* 173, no. 1 (1991).

36. Henry A. Giroux and Roger Simon, "Popular Culture and Critical Pedagogy: Everyday Life as a Basis for Curriculum Knowledge," in Henry Giroux and Peter McLaren, eds., *Critical Pedagogy, the State, and Cultural Struggle* (Albany: State University of New York Press, 1989), p. 239.

37. Joan Copjec, "The *Unvermögender* Other: Hysteria and Democracy in America," *New Formations*, no. 14 (1991): 40.

38. Ernesto Laclau, "Politics and the Limits of Modernity," in Andrew Ross, ed., *Universal Abandon? The Politics of Postmodernism* (Minneapolis: University of Minnesota Press, 1988), pp. 80–81.

39. Aronowitz and Giroux, *Postmodern Education*, p. 133.

40. Young, *White Mythologies*, p. 14.

41. Ibid., p. 16.

Chapter Four

Cultural Colonialism and Emancipation: Negotiating the Discourse of Freedom

EDUCATIONAL CHANGE IN POLAND

Education has always been a battlefield. Organizational and curricular changes brought about after World War II, when Eastern Europe was forced into the sphere of Soviet military and political control, were oriented toward some democratization of schooling. They opened up certain developmental possibilities for previously disadvantaged social groups. The reform was introduced in an atmosphere of "ideological offensive" against traditional educational attitudes. Education was supposed to "strengthen the foundations of the new socio-political reality: working class unity, workers' and peasants' alliance, and popular democracy."[1] Soon it proved, however, that education first of all had to serve the needs of Soviet colonization. Gradually, the whole school system was centralized, nationalized, and unified under a strict administrative control that deprived all social groups of any influence on what was going on in schools. Curricula, especially those that concerned social and historical issues, became oriented toward securing the Soviet-controlled Communist power. Socialism was presented as the final solution of all social problems; individual life was demonstrated as subordinated to the needs of broader social structures, especially—which may sound surprising in a colonized country— to the Nation. That paradox resulted from strong national feelings in Poland, strengthened by the experience of Nazi and Soviet occupations during the war. These feelings could not be denied, nor could they be ignored; they had to be colonized. Therefore, schools silenced the role of the USSR in the war of 1939 and stressed the cruelty of German occupation. The events of 1944– 1945, when the Soviets gained military and political control over the whole region, were presented as the final liberation and the turning point in the history of Poland, from then on secured from the German threat. That threat, of course, had to be kept alive, and so it was. Curricula presented the history of Poland as a history of wars fought against German aggressors and silenced hundreds of years of peaceful cooperation between the two nations. Hence education under the Soviet colonization proved to be somehow of nationalistic character. Thus reinforced, nationalism, along with the utopian vision of a just society introduced by the Communists in order to secure their political authority, played an important role in the revolutionary movement of Solidarity. (In chapter 1 I re- ferred to the phenomenon of antisocialist criticism concerning the "real" socialism, based upon socialist beliefs.)

The Communist rule in Poland did not end overnight, although one may easily point to some visible critical points in the history of the anti-Communist struggle, like massive strikes in 1980 or, more recently, round-table negotiations between the Communists and the democratic opposition and succeeding parliamentary elec- tions in 1989. In spite of the spectacular character of the events of that year, communism in Poland declined gradually, losing its power in subsequent areas of political life. It seems that Commu- nist education in Poland had its culmination in the 1970s, when the major educational reform aimed at implementation of a coherent and centrally manageable school system was undertaken. That was the peak of the Communist hegemony, the final attempt to make the educational (as well as the political) reality comply with Leninist ideals. In the late 1970s, when the general failure of these endeavors was clearly visible, a wave of alternative thinking surfaced, at first in academia, then in public media as well. Theorists reclaimed the silenced "humanist" and existential dimension of education and called for changes that would open up the possibilities of less restricted education for individual and social development. These endeavors, along with the wave of "popular education" (underground press, publications, and university lectures), constructed a cognitive background for the popular movement of the 1980s, when Solidarity created, for the first time since World War II, a viable alternative to the Communist rule.

The political breakthrough of 1980 (the Solidarity revolution following massive industrial actions) triggered a fundamental discussion on educational issues. Educational institutions were denounced as an element of the state's machinery that implemented its political goals and preserved the commonly disdained system. Teachers, parents, students, and communities started to reclaim their rights to influence schooling and thus subverted its mechanistic, bureaucratic, top-down organization. The most spectacular aspect of that movement emerged in the late 1980s, during the martial law that suppressed the process of political reforms and forced Solidarity to act underground, and concerned community-based schools. A parent in Krakow who won a case against educational authorities that struck down the requirement to send children to state-controlled schools opened up the way for small communities, teachers' associations, and individuals to organize schools and freely choose the best way of schooling for their children. The movement spread almost overnight to all major cities in the country and vastly contributed to the emergence of a new educational awareness. Education stopped being a synonym for political indoctrination and oppressive obligations and regained its positive meaning. However, parent-run and community-based schools represent only a small proportion of educational institutions, mostly due to financial problems—they are only partially supported by the state, and parents have to pay tuition. Still, they have contributed to the change of social attitudes to education.

The process of regaining the subjectivity, the agency, and the ability to act independently concerned all parties involved in the process of education. Teachers won significant union rights; students gained some legal protection securing their rights in schools. Recent political transformations have changed that situation in a somewhat paradoxical way. The end of communism brought about democratic changes in all spheres of social life, but social groups lost their sole responsibility for the reorganization of the system. It has become institutionalized, inscribed into governmental projects and schemes, and planned and implemented in an administrative manner. Reconstruction became a goal of the state rather than a popular movement. Moreover, the reconstruction is inevitably painful and prompts popular resistance in some of the most affected groups.[2] The school administration faces the problem of withdrawing recently granted teachers' union rights and increasing the work hours because the devastated state budget cannot bear the present financial burden. Quite paradoxically, the Ministry of Education meets some resistance from teachers who seem not to want to be free. The general direction of educational reform implies a reduction of obligatory curriculum content and aims at providing teachers with more freedom and more personal responsibility for what they teach. Teachers, however, often feel quite uncomfortable with the idea of being deprived of the safety guaranteed to them by state-controlled and obligatory curricula. When the state stands for radical change, people tend to cling to the familiar, secure, and taken-for-granted. It seems that the drive for freedom, the most important propulsive factor in Poland's recent history, met its limits when the state took over the power and responsibility to implement its ideals. This political issue is directly linked to the problem of identity.

POLITICS: DIFFERENCE AND HEGEMONY

As I have already said, the world described in postmodern theory is demonstrated as ontologically open and socially, provisionally closed. It is, as Ernesto Laclau puts it, radically contingent, driven by external antagonisms that cannot be resolved in any kind of dialectical synthesis, and it is being closed by numerous attempts at hegemonization, at giving it a conceivable shape through ideological and mythological practices.[3] These attempts are of particular importance in the discourse of freedom. In Eastern Europe, where the struggle against Communist totalitarianism employed a range of modernist myths,[4] the notion of freedom has been directly linked to that of autonomy. This perspective implies, on its part, a notion of identity, of a unified, identified, autonomous, separate subject—be it an individual or a community, a social class or a nation. As I tried to show in chapter 1, social identity in Communist Poland was shaped, most of all, by the dualistic distinction between "us" and "them" grounded in the uneven access to political power. As the vast majority felt disempowered in the totalitarian state, it was easy to form a unitary collective identity perceived as a potential subject of freedom. That collective subject ("us," "the nation," "the people") consisted of individual subjects identified around their "private" spaces and did not include any significant social identifications of a "middle range" concerning bigger social groups. The struggle for freedom was thought to accomplish the autonomy of all identified subjects (that is, of the nation and of individuals), and it developed a powerful strategy of solidarity. The moment of victory, however, made the issue of difference a priority. Deprived of "them," as well as of social (class) divisions typical of Western societies, people started to search for "other Others" in order to identify their collective subjectivity. They had no other choice but to turn to the sphere of myth and mystification. They became vulnerable to all possible strategies of othering: to nationalism, xenophobia, and religious fundamentalism. In order to be free in the modernist, and at the same time militant, meaning of the word, capable of inspiring people to fight for their rights, we have to sense who we are, who is the subject of freedom. The modernist notion of freedom is linked to the idea of unified subject. It is a colonial idea, craving for the Other, for exclusions, for certainty, and for mythological closures. Otherwise it does not exist; it cannot be accomplished. Perhaps this is one of the reasons

why there is so much dissatisfaction in all post-Communist societies. Economic hardships can be endured when people see sense
to them, and it is sense that is scarce, as people have ceased to
understand who they are.

It seems that two ways of coping with that crisis of meaning are
visible in the contemporary politics of identity. The first relies on
the search for scapegoats, for others who, when found and sacri-
ficed, can bring about unity in disintegrated societies. The anti-
Semitism that surfaced during the presidential campaign in Poland
in 1991, ethnic wars in Eastern and Southern Europe, the split of
Czechoslovakia, the rage about "secret agents" of the former
political police, racial tensions and conflicts with ethnic minorities
all over the region, and aggression against HIV patients all seem
to serve well as integrating factors in local communities and
sometimes, too, on national political scenes, where fears and the
dynamics of "othering" are played upon by politicians fighting for
popular support. That fight is itself a part of the second mechanism,
the drive for discursive hegemony. In Poland all the political parties
that emerged in the process of the differentiation of Solidarity try
to impose their definition of reality as the dominant political
discourse. In these attempts differentiation keeps dominating over
integration. Especially the political Right, which claims its prerog-
atives to hegemony as the major power succeeding the Communists, indulges in a festival of differences quite similar to that taking
place on the Left in Western societies,[5] making any viable political
coalition practically impossible. In the discursive vacuum that
results, on the one hand, from the inability of the Right to provide
a coherent political agenda and, on the other, from the exhaustion
of the discourse of the Left, discredited during the Communist
domination, the hegemonizing role is played by various kinds of
popular fundamentalism. First of all, the vacuum is being filled by
the Catholic church, overtly taking sides in the political struggle,
undertaking an educational offensive (lessons on religion have
been introduced to public schools), and trying to force anti-abor-
tion regulations. Another visible discourse claiming hegemony in
the crisis of identity of the early 1990s is nationalism, employed

by the most radical factions of the Right. Their plea for national independence, although it speaks to popular sentiments shaped by resistance against the Soviet domination, is clearly oriented against the vision of European integration as an agenda of social-democratic and liberal parties.

These three discourses make up a particular map of colonization: Christian fundamentalism and nationalism constitute an "internal" colonizing force, whereas the idea of a unified Europe and ambitions to join the EEC refer to the desire of superficial westernization developed during the political isolation of Eastern Europe and thus, in a way, contribute to some kind of cultural colonization. On the one hand, it is feared that European integration will limit the newly won national independence, and its antagonists raise questions of the economic colonization of Poland by foreign capital. The discourse of the Right counters the vision of a unified Europe with the idea of cultural and economic sovereignty applying to nationalistic myths, legitimized by the catchword of a "Europe of Nations." The cultural difference between Poland and Western societies is sometimes presented by the extreme Right as cultural superiority: Christian nationalists foretell a new crusade against the liberalism and moral relativism of the West and dream that Poland has a major role to play in a new Christianization of Europe. On the other hand, the idea of a unified Europe and the perspective of Poland joining the EEC speak to another mythological sphere, namely, the one of the Western lifestyle. "The surface of the West" (advertising and the consumer-goods market, fashion, American soap operas on TV, Coke and potato chips, and so on) has settled down for good in Central Europe and slowly, yet inevitably, covers up what used to be a visual basis of cultural identity. As I argued in previous chapters, looks are an important factor of identity construction, and we do not look much different. The ideological conflict, therefore, is played out between the surface and the foundations, and it is a conflict between two hegemonizing claims, two discourses of colonization. One operates from the surface and employs a mosaic of diversified details tacitly changing the cultural identity; the other operates from "below," from the dark, mythical foundations of the Nation in a Christian disguise, and uses more or less subtle techniques of "othering," stretching from refined philosophical disputes on the specificity of the Polish culture and theological arguments against Western relativism to xenophobic anti-German, anti-Russian, anti-Jewish, and anti-Every-Other assaults.

The reality is constituted in between: between the surface and the depth, between the national and the cosmopolitan, between hegemonizing narratives. Postmodernism dismissed the hopes for the social structure to constitute "itself" in the course of some evolutionary changes of objective processes, and thus it opened up a sphere of new responsibilities for purely human, discursive actions and disclosed a new dimension of freedom, this time not a freedom of unified subjects, not a freedom of hegemonized identities. It is a peculiar, postmodern freedom to shape the social reality in discursive practices. If this freedom is to be accomplished, it demands another freedom: a freedom from hegemonized, taken-for-granted identities, a paradoxical freedom from identity that challenges the whole sphere of politics and education.

THE PARADOX OF EMANCIPATION

I am analyzing the relations between Central and Eastern Europe and the West as if these regions were to encounter each other for the first time in their history. That, of course, is an absurdity, yet the present situation calls for stressing the new elements in mutual relations between the countries previously isolated by the Iron Curtain, favors a kind of oblivion of historical traditions, and permits treating the present relations as an encounter of Others, as a play of differences rather than a reconciliation of two halves of the same old continent. These relations are in every aspect ambivalent: first, because of the "knowledge gap" resulting from almost half a century of isolation. We have to learn a lot about our respective other cultures and to relate that learning to old stereotypes frozen in our collective memories. Second, we must deal with the complex character of cultural transmission and the ambiguity of the culture itself. What can be characterized by the notion of postmodernity is, at the same time, modern in numerous aspects; cultures that colonize poorer societies at the same time carry with them possibilities of emancipation from the very same dependence. The modern notion of freedom conceived as autonomy, implying exclusions and colonial domination, at the same time presupposes an idea of tolerance calling for mutual understanding and nonviolent relations between cultures. In this context the idea of emancipation, transmitted eastward with the whole baggage of postmodernity, shows its peculiar ambivalence. Western emancipatory theories are sometimes considered empowering in the discourse of the East trying to salvage some of its identity against Western cultural domination—a truly postcolonial ambiguity.

The ambivalence of cultural relations, and hence of the whole process of the construction of identity, is clearly visible within the discourse of postmodernity, inevitably entangled in the discussion with modernity and embracing its fundamental categories. Modernity—the dominant discourse of the West, defining its cultural identity—produces exclusions. These exclusions, objectified in the form of "colonial Others," in turn challenge the dominant discourse and open up the sphere of displacements and differentiations within the West.[6] Modernity ruptures its own cultural codes; it produces postmodernity. The ambivalence is also visible within the discourse of freedom (exclusions and "othering" as foundations of the autonomy of the subject) and within the discourse of the nation (as Homi Bhabha has it, the nation is a narrative, a mythological closure, and at the same time it produces a powerful creative potential of the culture.)[7] The construction of identity, and therefore of politics, and therefore of education, takes place in a space of ambivalence, of translations, of negotiations. It is a play between contingent openness and ideological closures, between democratic possibilities and totalitarian certainty, between superficial differences and fundamental sameness. Identity is constructed in a play in which one of the main roles is performed by identity itself, in a play against identity.

NEGOTIATING THE DISCOURSE OF
FREEDOM: EDUCATION AGAINST IDENTITY?

Just when I am trying to conclude this book, a political battle is going on in Poland. This time it is a peculiar battle setting all ideologies against a newly emerging kind of social pragmatism. I could not expect to be challenged by the political context of my writing more fundamentally; I could not think of a more demanding situation in which to write this book. The ideologies that brought communism to its end—nationalism, Christian fundamentalism, liberal individualism, even the ethos of solidarity—facing the lack of the common enemy, have engaged in a merciless quarrel about which of the former combatant discourses has a better right to define the sphere of the political. As a result, they all have lost. No one of them is capable of hegemonizing the flux of reality; no one is able to gain significant popular support. Yet the "postcolonial desire,"—the desire of decolonized society for an identity,[8] feeds that discursive battle and legitimizes all attempts to dominate the cultural scene with one pervasive definition of reality. The problem with this struggle for hegemony and identity is that all parties involved subsequently lose their credibility and bring the discourses they employ to political death. All modernist "master categories" of the hardly completed struggle for political freedom annihilate one another, and political authorities perish in the indignity of mutual denigration. Moreover, there is hardly any position in sight from which the task of negotiation could be initiated—or rather, there is one, but it cannot be fully articulated because it is attempting to formulate itself as a purely anti-ideological position of social pragmatism. Pragmatic philosophy does not practically exist in Eastern Europe; it has not settled down in the region, whose fundamental task was to resist domination and retain cultural identity. That could only be accomplished through highly abstract, utopian ideologies, remote from reality, speaking to metaphorical social imagination. Pragmatic concentration on the tasks of social life, as a result, is lacking a conceptual background. It cannot join the political discussion as a legitimate discourse. Its language is alien to almost everybody on the political scene.[9] Perhaps that is its ambiguous advantage that should be taken up in educational practice.

The sphere of the practical situates itself always between conceptual articulations, always beyond the range of discursive systems. Reality, with its dimensions of practical life, cannot be fully narratized, even though its narratization is a prior aim of discursive practices. Narration is an ambiguous enterprise. Discursive actions are practices themselves, and their inability to grasp the sphere of the practical means, as well, that one cannot achieve self-consciousness on the discursive level. Their constant entanglement in conceptual schemes, with their dualistic structuralizations that make the task of discursive self-consciousness practically impossible, creates a rupture, a distance enabling a particular sphere of critique, and constructs a prior difference of signifiers and the signified within the very sphere of discourse. Within the discursive sphere the practical plays the role of the undecidable, of a "third" dimension of all conceptual dualisms. This aspect of the practical has been realized in the philosophy of language even before deconstructionism. Let us quote, for instance, from Mieczyslaw Krapiec, a Polish philosopher working within the tradition of classical metaphysics:

What is particularly interesting is that in conceptual cognition we basically grasp the extreme states as subjects of relations, towards which our intellectual attention is oriented. For it is so that we do not describe a given feature of the thing in its positive aspects, but rather a feature as it counters another feature, or correlates with it. Features—elements of things— grasped positively and directly are those only which relate to the utilitarian dimension of things. In relation to the use of things, to their instrumental handling, we cognize things positively, e.g. in a measurable way. Cognition not related to the use of things is—as it has been said—grasping their extreme states, stating how a feature is different from its negation, how far it is situated from what it is not. Here we

have a specifically human process of cognition of the being
on the background of the negation of not-being.[10]

Knowing the practical is, therefore, a particular act of cognition,
different from "specifically human" conceptual dualism. It is no
wonder, then, that in the discursive struggle, inevitably stretching
itself between polarized dichotomies, the sphere of practical knowing can play a deconstructive, liberating role and provide for a
standing from which to interrogate all ideological positions. That
pragmatic trace of emancipatory thinking is well recognized in
American radical theory (it suffices to mention Cornel West's
argument linking postmodernism and pragmatism, or Nancy
Fraser's notion of a "democratic-socialist-feminist pragmatism").[11] What is important is that knowing the practical is also an
intellectual, conceptual endeavor; it has its abstract dimension. As
conceptual cognition, it may also serve the need of identification—
a particular identification, different from the one grounded in the
practice of othering. Concepts referring to the sphere of the practical do not need their negations in order to identify aspects of
reality. Can this feature of practical knowledge be effectively used
in the practice of identity formation, in education?

The present situation creates a fundamental challenge to critical
education in Poland, previously shaped by the task of resisting the
monopoly of the Communist discourse in social life. That meant
questioning the dominant ideology on its own grounds, disclosing
its silenced dimensions, countering its hegemony with other discourses, and creating a sphere of counterdiscursive ideological
articulations. In other words, at stake was the issue of ideological
differentiation. The contemporary political scene, however, poses
a fundamentally new challenge to critical educators. The critique
of ideology is far from sufficient, as it may merely counter one
hegemony with other ideological claims. That would be futile, as
in the present situation all ideologies are clearly partial and unable
to construct the sphere of the social. Moreover, they are suspected
of creating distorted images of social life; they are read as discursive practices aimed at distracting public attention from dramatic

issues of poverty, unemployment, and the lack of developmental chances for the young generation and of security for the old. These issues, traditionally belonging to the agenda of the Left, have been deprived of their legitimate articulations in the course of the anti-Communist revolution. As a result, there is no political power that would risk raising these questions without facing incriminating charges of bringing back the old political order, which was using the discourse of social justice as a cover for totalitarian rule. Needed is a particular strategy of identity construction, a strategy that defers the postcolonial desire, detours quick-fix identifications around oppositional, dualistic concepts, and distances itself from hegemonizing claims of traditional ideologies. Needed is an anti-dualistic education that delays the possibility of closures, an education that could do without the practice of othering. Ideologies, closures, and social structures constructed in discursive practices are necessary. They are of prior importance if a society is to be able to communicate and undertake collective actions. But ideologies must be open to interrogation; closures must be understood as provisional and pragmatic; social structures must be understood as discursively constructed. It seems that such education can be grounded in the sphere of practical social experiences. Practical concepts do not demand that "other" concepts be formed. Identifications constructed around social needs and practical collective actions do not demand "other" social subjects; they do not have to be aimed at construction and subsequent appropriation of the Other. Such education can be grounded in the ethics of solidarity and difference; it can open the sphere of the social to different articulations, to otherness that is not utilized in the practice of identification.

Certainly, the practice of identification based on practical experiences and social needs is more difficult, in a way less attractive, and definitely less effective in terms of providing long-lasting results enclosing the world in clear-cut cognitive frames than the one grounded in conceptual oppositions. But it is difficult to imagine a more convincing demonstration of the need of such education than the present political situation in Central and Eastern

Europe, where ideological identifications (like those built around the ideas of the nation, or religion, or rights) brought about an ultimate differentiation that practically closed all possibilities of discursive hegemony, and therefore, as Ernesto Laclau puts it, of constructing the sphere of the social.[12]

It seems that the only way out of that ideological standstill is through the sphere of the practical, and that those societies that find the strength to overcome their desire for identity will eventually find their relatively secure place in the postmodern world. In chapter 1 of this book I wrote that pragmatism is a privilege of those cultures that identify themselves with the stronger, "better" side of conceptual structuralizations, whereas those that are marginalized, identified as supplementary "others," build their identities in the schizoid sphere of the dream of "being the Other" (the "big" other, the colonizing other). In this context the challenge of pragmatism I am writing about is doubly paradoxical. First, pragmatism seems impossible on the part of those who survived political domination owing to their power of dreaming. Second, in the new political context, pragmatism is just another colonial discourse; it is the dominant discourse of the West. To resist the "postcolonial desire" for identity that is pushing the region to political instability and civil wars, the decolonized East of Europe now has to face the challenge of another colonization.

The challenge of pragmatism is a question of translation; the postcolonial identity is a question of negotiation. Education in Central and Eastern Europe faces the most difficult problem of keeping itself in the fragile sphere of openness, interrogation, and translation, in the sphere where meanings and subjectivities are being constructed rather than identified and transmitted. This is the sphere of freedom: the sphere not determined, not frozen in ideological closures. Postmodern and postcolonial education is, therefore, an education in freedom rather than for freedom. The latter would imply some kind of ontological autonomy, and that in turn would have to construct and appropriate the sphere of otherness. Educating in freedom, in a world open to all identifications and vulnerable to all possible closures, we have to educate for responsibility, for solidarity, for ethical openness to the others, and for abilities to actively construct reality. We have to defer the desire of identity. Leaving identity open to negotiation, keeping it in the sphere of constant provisionality and within the process of translation, seems to be the only possibility of preventing ourselves from a slippage into colonial dependence and totalitarian certainty.

NOTES

1. Stanislaw Mausenberg, *Reforma szkolnictwa w Polsce w latach 1944–1948* (Wroclaw: Ossolineum, 1984), p. 182; my translation.

2. Note, for instance, the situation in industry. The state-owned heavy industry was set up in order to provide goods mainly for the already nonexistent Soviet military sector. That industry is economically ineffective and cannot be privatized (there is nobody who would like to buy an obsolete steel mill). It employs a vast number of workers; moreover, it used to be the biggest taxpayer, and therefore its decline affects the whole state economy. It has to be liquidated in some way, but nobody has found a safe way of doing it.

3. Ernesto Laclau, *New Reflections on the Revolution of Our Time* (London: Verso, 1990), pp. 89–93.

4. This aspect of modern ideology has been noticed by Henry Giroux: "Postmodernism and feminism have challenged modernism on a variety of theoretical and political fronts . . . , but there is another side to modernism that has expressed itself more recently in the ongoing struggles in Eastern Europe." Henry A. Giroux, "Modernism, Postmodernism, and Feminism: Rethinking the Boundaries of Educational Discourse," in Henry A. Giroux, ed., *Postmodernism, Feminism, and Cultural Politics: Redrawing Educational Boundaries* (Albany: State University of New York Press, 1991), p. 2.

5. See, for example, Kobena Mercer, "Welcome to the Jungle: Identity and Diversity in Postmodern Politics," in Jonathan Rutherford, ed., *Identity: Community, Culture, Difference* (London: Lawrence and Wishart, 1990).

6. See Robert Young, *White Mythologies: Writing History and the West* (London: Routledge, 1990).

7. "For the nation, as a form of cultural elaboration (in the Gramscian sense) is an agency of *ambivalent* narration that holds culture at its

most productive position, as a force for subordination, fracturing, diffusing, reproducing, as much as producing, creating, forcing, guiding." Homi Bhabha, "Introduction," in Homi Bhabha, ed., *Nation and Narration* (London: Routledge, 1990), pp. 3–4.

8. I am using the notion of postcolonial desire after Peter McLaren, who borrows the term from Simon During. Peter McLaren, "Post-Colonial Pedagogy: Post-Colonial Desire and Decolonized Community," *Education and Society* 9, no. 2 (1991): 135–58.

9. For the first time this kind of pragmatic articulation appeared in the agenda formulated by Waldemar Pawlak, designated prime minister in June 1992. In his fruitless attempts to construct the government, Pawlak overtly refused to engage in ideological battles and tried to create a formula of cooperation on the basis of solving practical problems of the society.

10. Mieczyslaw Krapiec, *Jezyk i swiat realny* (Lublin: Redakcja Wydawnictw Katolickiego Uniwersytetu Lubelskiego, 1985), p. 85; my translation.

11. Anders Stephanson, "Interview with Cornel West," in Andrew Ross, ed., *Universal Abandon? The Politics of Postmodernism* (Minneapolis: University of Minnesota Press, 1988) pp. 269–273; Nancy Fraser, *Unruly Practices: Power, Discourse, and Gender in Contemporary Social Theory* (Minneapolis: University of Minnesota Press, 1989), p. 6.

12. Laclau, *New Reflections on the Revolution of Our Time*, pp. 89–93.

Selected Bibliography

America 2000: An Education Strategy. Washington D.C.: U.S. Department of Education, 1991.

Aronowitz, Stanley. "Postmodernism and Politics." In Andrew Ross, ed., *Universal Abandon? The Politics of Postmodernism.* Minneapolis: University of Minnesota Press, 1988, pp. 46–62.

Aronowitz, Stanley, and Henry A. Giroux. *Postmodern Education: Politics, Culture, and Social Criticism.* Minneapolis: University of Minnesota Press, 1991.

Avens, Roberts. *The New Gnosis: Heidegger, Hillman, and Angels.* Dallas: Spring Publications, 1984.

Bauman, Zygmunt. *Freedom.* Minneapolis: University of Minnesota Press, 1988.

Bhabha, Homi. "The Commitment to Theory." *New Formations*, no. 5 (Summer 1988): 5–23.

Bhabha, Homi, ed. *Nation and Narration.* London and New York: Routledge, 1990.

Bhabha, Homi. "The Third Space." In Jonathan Rutherford, ed., *Identity: Community, Culture, Difference.* London: Lawrence and Wishart, 1990, pp. 207–221.

Bloom, Allan. *The Closing of the American Mind: How Higher Education Has Failed Democracy and Impoverished the Souls of Today's Students.* New York: Simon and Schuster, 1987.

Boyne, Roy, and Ali Rattansi, eds. *Postmodernism and Society*. New York: St. Martin's Press, 1990.

Carlson, Dennis. "Poststructuralism, Critical Curriculum Theorizing, and Social Movements." Paper delivered at the Bergamo Conference on Curriculum Theory and Classroom Practice. Dayton, Ohio, 1991.

Cherryholmes, Cleo. *Power and Criticism: Poststructural Investigations in Education*. New York: Teachers College Press, Columbia University, 1988.

Connor, Steven. *Postmodernist Culture: An Introduction to Theories of the Contemporary*. New York: Basil Blackwell, 1989.

Copjec, Joan. "The *Unvermögender* Other: Hysteria and Democracy in America." *New Formations*, no. 14 (1991): 29–41.

Derrida, Jacques. "Deconstruction and the Other." In Richard Kearney, *Dialogues with Contemporary Continental Thinkers: The Phenomenological Heritage*. Manchester, England: Manchester University Press, 1984, pp. 107–126.

Derrida, Jacques. *Margins of Philosophy*. Translated by Alan Bass. Chicago: University of Chicago Press, 1982.

Derrida, Jacques. *Of Grammatology*. Translated by Gayatri Ch. Spivak. Baltimore: Johns Hopkins University Press, 1976.

Derrida, Jacques. *Positions*. Translated by Alan Bass. Chicago: University of Chicago Press, 1981.

Dolar, Mladen. "The Legacy of the Enlightenment: Foucault and Lacan." *New Formations*, no. 14 (1991): 43–56.

Doll, William E., Jr. "Foundations for a Post-Modern Curriculum." *Journal of Curriculum Studies* 21, no. 3 (1989): 243–253.

Foucault, Michel. "The Political Technology of Individuals." In L. H. Martin, H. Gutman, and P. H. Hutton, eds. *Technologies of the Self: A Seminar with Michel Foucault*. Amherst: University of Massachusetts Press, 1988, pp. 145–162.

Foucault, Michel. *Power/Knowledge: Selected Interviews and Other Writings, 1972–1977*. New York: Pantheon Books, 1980.

Fraser, Nancy. "Rethinking the Public Sphere: A Contribution to the Critique of Actually Existing Democracy." *Social Text,* no. 25/26 (1990): 56–80.

Fraser, Nancy. *Unruly Practices: Power, Discourse, and Gender in Contemporary Social Theory*. Minneapolis: University of Minnesota Press, 1989.

Gay, Peter. "Freud and Freedom: On a Fox in Hedgehog's Clothing." In Alan Ryan, ed., *The Idea of Freedom*. Oxford: Oxford University Press, 1979.

Giroux, Henry A. *Border Crossings: Cultural Workers and the Politics of Education*. New York: Routledge, 1992.

Giroux, Henry A. "Educational Leadership and the Crisis of Democratic Culture." Address delivered at the University Council for Educational Administration Annual Conference, Baltimore, Maryland, 1991.

Giroux, Henry A. "Post-Colonial Ruptures and Democratic Possibilities: Multiculturalism as Anti-Racist Pedagogy." *Cultural Critique*, no. 21 (Spring 1992).

Giroux, Henry A., ed. *Postmodernism, Feminism, and Cultural Politics: Redrawing Educational Boundaries*. Albany: State University of New York Press, 1991.

Giroux, Henry A. *Schooling and the Struggle for Public Life: Critical Pedagogy in the Modern Age*. Minneapolis: University of Minnesota Press, 1988.

Giroux, Henry A. "Theories of Reproduction and Resistance in the New Sociology of Education." *Harvard Educational Review* 53, no. 3, (1983): 257–293.

Giroux, Henry A. *Theory and Resistance in Education*. South Hadley, Mass.: Bergin and Garvey, 1983.

Giroux, Henry A., and Peter McLaren, eds. *Critical Pedagogy, the State, and Cultural Struggle*. Albany: State University of New York Press, 1989.

Giroux, Henry A., and Peter McLaren. "Language, Schooling, and Subjectivity: Beyond a Pedagogy of Reproduction and Resistance." In K. Borman, P. Swami, and L. Wagstaff, eds., *Contemporary Issues in U.S. Education*. Norwood, N.J.: Ablex Publishing Corporation, 1991, pp. 61–83.

Giroux, Henry A., and David Trend. "Cultural Workers, Pedagogy, and the Politics of Difference: Beyond Cultural Conservatism." *Cultural Studies* 6, no. 1 (1992).

Gough, Noel. "From Epistemology to Ecopolitics: Renewing the Paradigm for Curriculum." *Journal of Curriculum Studies* 21, no. 3 (1989): pp. 225–241.

Greene, Maxine. *The Dialectic of Freedom*. New York: Teachers College Press, 1988.

Grossberg, Lawrence. "Teaching the Popular." In Cary Nelson, ed., *Theory in the Classroom*. Urbana: University of Illinois Press, 1986, pp. 177–200.

Grossberg, Lawrence. *We Gotta Get Out of This Place: Popular Conservatism and Postmodern Culture*. New York: Routledge, 1992.

Hall, Stuart, and Martin Jacques, eds. *New Times: The Changing Face of Politics in the 1990s*. London: Verso, 1990.

Hassan, Ihab. *Paracriticisms. Seven Speculations of the Times*. Urbana: University of Illinois Press, 1975.

Heidegger, Martin. *Schelling's Treatise on the Essence of Human Freedom*. Athens: Ohio University Press, 1985.

Hutcheon, Linda. *The Politics of Postmodernism*. London: Routledge, 1989.

Ingarden, Roman. *Man and Value*. München: Philosophia Verlag, 1983.

Jameson, Frederic. "Postmodernism, or the Cultural Logic of Late Capitalism." *New Left Review*, no. 146 (July–August 1984): 53–92.

Lacan, Jacques. *The Four Fundamental Concepts of Psycho-analysis*. New York: W. W. Norton, 1981.

Laclau, Ernesto. *New Reflections on the Revolution of Our Time*. London: Verso, 1990.

Lankshear, Colin. *Freedom and Education*. Auckland: Milton Brookes Publications, 1982.

Lather, Pati. "Postmodernism and the Politics of Enlightenment." *Educational Foundations* 3, no. 3 (Fall 1989): 7–28.

McLaren, Peter. "Critical Pedagogy: Constructing an Arch of Social Dreaming and a Doorway to Hope." *Journal of Education* 173, no. 1 (1991): pp. 9–34.

McLaren, Peter. "Post-Colonial Pedagogy: Post-Colonial Desire and Decolonized Community." *Education and Society* 9, no. 2 (1991): 135–158.

McLaren, Peter. *Schooling as a Ritual Performance: Towards a Political Economy of Educational Symbols and Gestures*. London: Routledge and Kegan Paul, 1986.

McLaren, Peter, and Rhonda Hammer. "Critical Pedagogy and the Postmodern Challenge: Toward a Critical Postmodernist Pedagogy of Liberation." *Educational Foundations* 3, no. 3, (Fall 1989): 29–62.

Mouffe, Chantal. "Hegemony and New Political Subjects: Toward a New Concept of Democracy." In Cary Nelson and Lawrence Grossberg, eds., *Marxism and the Interpretation of Culture.* Urbana: University of Illinois Press, 1988.

Nelson, Cary, ed. *Theory in the Classroom.* Urbana: University of Illinois Press, 1986.

Rogers, Carl. *Freedom to Learn for the 80's.* Columbus, Ohio: Charles E. Merrill, 1983.

Ross, Andrew, ed. *Universal Abandon? The Politics of Postmodernism.* Minneapolis: University of Minnesota Press, 1988.

Rutherford, Jonathan, ed. *Identity: Community, Culture, Difference.* London: Lawrence and Wishart, 1990.

Ryan, Michael. *Marxism and Deconstruction: A Critical Articulation.* Baltimore: Johns Hopkins University Press, 1982.

Sarup, Madan. *An Introductory Guide to Post-structuralism and Postmodernism.* Athens: University of Georgia Press, 1989.

Scholes, Robert. *Textual Power: Literary Theory and the Teaching of English.* New Haven, Conn.: Yale University Press, 1985.

Simon, Roger. "For a Pedagogy of Possibility." *Critical Pedagogy Networker* 1, no. 1 (1988): 1–4.

Slaughter, Richard A. "Cultural Reconstruction in the Postmodern World." *Journal of Curriculum Studies* 21, no. 3 (1989): pp. 255–270.

Solomon-Godeau, Abigail. *Photography at the Dock: Essays on Photographic History, Institutions, and Practices.* Minneapolis: University of Minnesota Press, 1991.

Spivak, Gayatri Ch. "Can the Subaltern Speak? Speculations on Widow-Sacrifice." *Wedge*, no. 7/8 (Winter–Spring 1985): 120–130.

Spivak, Gayatri Ch. "Neocolonialism and the Secret Agent of Knowledge." *Oxford Literary Review* 13, no. 1/2 (1991): pp. 220–251.

Spivak, Gayatri Ch. *The Post-Colonial Critic: Interviews, Strategies, Dialogues.* Edited by Sarah Harasym. New York: Routledge, 1990.

Stephanson, Anders. "Interview with Cornel West." In Andrew Ross, ed., *Universal Abandon? The Politics of Postmodernism.* Minneapolis: University of Minnesota Press, 1988, pp. 269–286.

Ulmer, Gregory. *Applied Grammatology: Post(e)-Pedagogy from Jacques Derrida to Joseph Beuys.* Baltimore: Johns Hopkins University Press, 1985.

Ulmer, Gregory. *Teletheory: Grammatology in the Age of Video.* New York: Routledge, 1989.

Willis, Paul. *Learning to Labor: How Working Class Kids Get Working Class Jobs.* New York: Columbia University, 1981.

Witkowski, Lech. *Uniwersalizm pogranicza: O semiotyce kultury Michala Bachtina w kontekscie edukacji.* Torun: Adam Marszalek, 1991.

Young, Robert. *White Mythologies: Writing History and the West.* London: Routledge, 1990.

Zagumenov, Uri L. "In the High Hope of Cooperation." Paper delivered at the University Council for Educational Administration Annual Conference, Baltimore, Maryland, 1991.

Index

About the Author

TOMASZ SZKUDLAREK is Assistant Professor in the Institute of Education at the University of Gdansk in Poland. He has written books on critical pedagogy published in Poland and numerous articles in educational journals.